The Dress of Women

Recent Titles in
Contributions in Women's Studies

On Top of the World: Women's Political Leadership in Scandinavia and Beyond
Bruce O. Solheim

Victorian London's Middle-Class Housewife: What She Did All Day
Yaffa Claire Draznin

Connecting Links: The British and American Woman Suffrage Movements, 1900–1914
Patricia Greenwood Harrison

Female Journeys: Autobiographical Expressions by French and Italian Women
Claire Marrone

Excluded from Suffrage History: Matilda Joslyn Gage, Nineteenth-Century American Feminist
Leila R. Brammer

The Artist as Outsider in the Novels of Toni Morrison and Virginia Woolf
Lisa Williams

(Out) Classed Women: Contemporary Chicana Writers on Inequitable Gendered Power Relations
Phillipa Kafka

"Saddling La Gringa": Gatekeeping in Literature by Contemporary Latina Writers
Phillipa Kafka

Representing the Marginal Woman in Nineteenth-Century Russian Literature: Personalism, Feminism, and Polyphony
Svetlana Slavskaya Grenier

From the Field to the Legislature: A History of Women in the Virgin Islands
Eugenia O'Neal

Women and Domestic Experience in Victorian Political Fiction
Susan Johnston

African American Women and Social Action: The Clubwomen and Volunteerism from Jim Crow to the New Deal 1896–1936
Floris Barnett Cash

The Dress of Women

A Critical Introduction to the Symbolism and Sociology of Clothing

Charlotte Perkins Gilman

Edited, with an introduction by
Michael R. Hill and Mary Jo Deegan

Contributions in Women's Studies, Number 193

GREENWOOD PRESS
Westport, Connecticut • London

Library of Congress Cataloging-in-Publication Data

Gilman, Charlotte Perkins, 1860–1935.
The dress of women : a critical introduction to the symbolism and sociology of clothing / Charlotte Perkins Gilman ; edited, with an introduction by Michael R. Hill and Mary Jo Deegan.
p. cm.—(Contributions in women's studies, ISSN 0147–104X ; no. 193)
"Originally published in Gilman's monthly journal, The forerunner, in 1915"—Introd.
Includes bibliographical references and index.
ISBN 0–313–31270–2 (alk. paper)
1. Sociology—Methodology. 2. Sociology—Philosophy. 3. Gilman, Charlotte Perkins, 1860–1935—Contributions in sociology. 4. Costume—Symbolic aspects. 5. Clothing and dress—Psychological aspects. I. Hill, Michael R. II. Deegan, Mary Jo, 1946– III. Title. IV. Series.
HM511.G55 2002
301'.01—dc21 2001023884

British Library Cataloguing in Publication Data is available.

Library of Congress Catalog Card Number: 2001023884
ISBN: 0–313–31270–2
ISSN: 0147–104X

First published in 2002

Greenwood Press, 88 Post Road West, Westport, CT 06881
An imprint of Greenwood Publishing Group, Inc.
www.greenwood.com

Printed in the United States of America

The paper used in this book complies with the Permanent Paper Standard issued by the National Information Standards Organization (Z39.48–1984).

10 9 8 7 6 5 4 3 2

This edition
is dedicated to
Margaret Ellen Hilligoss Ishikawa
and Wesley H. Ishikawa—
distinguished professors, social workers,
aunt and uncle extraordinaire,
and to the memory of
George Elliott Howard
(1849–1928),
Nebraska sociologist and president of the
American Sociological Society,
in whose personal copies of *The Forerunner*
we found the text of
The Dress of Women.

Contents

Introduction: Charlotte Perkins Gilman on the Symbolism and Sociology of Clothing

Michael R. Hill and Mary Jo Deegan

In *The Dress of Women*, Charlotte Perkins Gilman presents a nonfiction analysis of the symbolism and sociology of clothing. Originally published in Gilman's monthly journal, *The Forerunner*, in 1915, *The Dress of Women* was serialized, month by month, at the same time as Gilman's well-known novel, *Herland*, and a year prior to Gilman's companion work, *With Her In Ourland: Sequel to Herland. The Dress of Women*, published here for the first time in book form, is a lively, nonfiction guidebook to many of the gender issues presented in Gilman's Herland/Ourland saga and provides Gilman's intellectual, philosophical, and sociological insight into the ethical situations and plot developments that are simultaneously explored in her two didactic novels.

Beyond its interest to fans and scholars of the Herland/Ourland saga, however, *The Dress of Women* is, in its own right, a major analytical treatise by one of America's foremost sociological theorists: Charlotte Perkins Gilman. We have, as sociologists, added the subtitle, *A Critical Introduction to the Symbolism and Sociology of Clothing*, to emphasize Gilman's specifically sociological project in this work. Gilman critically and comprehensively analyzes the institutional generation and ideological support of gendered practices in the modern world, focussing on fashion and dress as paradigm examples. She marshals a well-developed holistic grasp of enduring, coercive institutional patterns and their interrelationships, and she astutely anticipates much that is considered novel in Erving Goffman's (1959) classic analyis of *The Presentation of Self in Everyday Life* and his otherwise insightful *Gender Advertisements* (1979). Gilman's adaptation and thorough-going extension of Thorstein Veblen's (1899b) *The Theory of the Leisure Class* places her among the leading critical social thinkers of the early twentieth century.

Gilman's insightful analyses remain astonishingly fresh, and *The Dress of Women* raises and dissects core issues that today, at the start of the twenty-first century, regularly find voice in women's magazines and on TV talk shows, including: "slavishly wearing the newest fashions," "comfortable clothes," "dressing to impress men," "the high cost of fashion," "impressing other women," "modesty in clothing," "dressing for success," "beauty in clothing," "sensible apparel," "the ethics of wearing fur," and so on. Many of the institutional and aesthetic questions that Gilman offers breezily in *Herland* and *With Her in Ourland* are here reiterated and given more formal thematic unity. But, here too, as in her fiction, Gilman's style is characterized by pert examples and acerbic wit. Below, we highlight Gilman's work in sociology, note her intellectual connections to Thorstein Veblen, and outline the linkage between cloth and clothing, as explicated in *The Dress of Women*, and the plot line in the Herland/Ourland narrative.

CHARLOTTE PERKINS GILMAN: SOCIOLOGIST

Gilman's (1935) autobiography, diaries (1994, 1998), love letters (1995), bibliography (Scharnhorst 1985b), first husband's diaries (Stetson 1985), and numerous literary studies and biographies (e.g., M. A. Hill 1980; Scharnhorst 1985a; Mayering 1989; Lane 1990; Karpinski 1992; Kessler 1995; Knight 1997; Rudd and Gough 1999; Knight 1999; Golden and Zangrando 2000) are well known, and her work specifically in sociology is slowly gaining wider, albeit belated, appreciation. The critique of Gilman's prolific work is a virtual industry among scholars in departments of English and modern languages, and—while undoubtedly relevant to textual studies—the large body of literary criticism obtains no discussion here, for our guiding interest is primarily sociological.

Scholars in disciplines cognate to sociology have championed Gilman, but with mixed results—sometimes damning Gilman with faint or convoluted praise. Carl Degler (1966) and William O'Neill (1972) are prime examples: these male historians kept Gilman's books alive in the 1960s and 1970s, but Lois N. Magner (1978: 70) shows that Degler exhibits an apparent "compulsion to issue warnings about taking her [Gilman's] claims to scientific background too seriously." Analogously, O'Neill (1972: xviii) condescendingly wrote that "Mrs. Gilman was, in her prime, the cleverest phrasemaker among leading feminists." Despite these limitations, however, O'Neill and Degler significantly contributed to Gilman scholarship by incorporating her in their other writings. O'Neill (1967) analyzed Gilman's role in changing ideas about divorce, the family, and the home. Degler (1989) re-introduced Gilman's social thought to a new generation of scholars. Andrew Sinclair (1966: 272), by contrast, is a stronger ally. He boldly and unambiguously claimed that Gilman was the "Marx and Veblen" of the woman's movement. Among other writers in cognate disciplines, Polly Wynn Allen's (1988) treatise on Gilman's architectural and domestic theories holds particular relevance for the social sciences.

Recent, specifically sociological writing on Gilman began with Alice S. Rossi (1973: 566–72) who, in *The Feminist Papers*, underscored Gilman's social critiques. Mary Jo Deegan (1981: 16) noted the influence on Gilman of the first president of the American Sociological Society, Lester Ward, and documented Gilman's early participation in the Society (now the American Sociological Association). James L. Terry (1983) argued for including Gilman's work in the sociology curriculum. Deegan (1987) included Gilman in a list of the top twenty-five most important women sociologists, noted Gilman's professional and personal friendship with Jane Addams, a Chicago sociologist (Deegan 1988: 229), and located Gilman's mature professional sociological career within the Golden Era of Women in Sociology (1890–1920), and her eclipse, after 1920, during the subsequent Dark Era of Patriarchal Ascendancy in which many women sociologists in the United States were reduced to near oblivion, at least within disciplinary sociology (Deegan 1991: 15–21). Bruce Keith (1991) succinctly surveyed Gilman's sociological contributions. Lemert (1997: 15–17) turned a sociological eye toward Gilman's early classic, *The Yellow Wall-Paper*. Pat Lengermann and Jill Niebrugge (1998: 105–48) devote a full chapter of their text/reader to Gilman's treatment of gender and social structure. Michael R. Hill (1996) sketches the sociological dimensions of *Herland*, and Deegan (1997) details at some length the philosophical and theoretical framework of *With Her in Ourland: Sequel to Herland*. R. A. Sydie and Bert

Adams (forthcoming) offer a critical comparison between the sociologies of Gilman and Beatrice Webb. Deegan and Christopher Podeschi (forthcoming) document that Gilman was an historical founder of "ecofeminist pragmatism" who anticipated many positions found in ecofeminist writing today. In short, several sociologists are taking Charlotte Perkins Gilman seriously, *as a sociologist.*

Gilman was a well-known sociologist in her era. She presented review papers at the annual meetings of the American Sociological Society (Gilman 1907a, b), an organization of which she was a dues-paying member, and published full-length articles in the *American Journal of Sociology* (Gilman 1908, 1909). Leading American sociologists—Lester Ward, Edward A. Ross, Jane Addams, and others—considered her a friend and a colleague (Deegan 1997: 12–26). As a pedagogue, however, Gilman pursued the popular lecture circuit and the lay press rather than the classroom or the specialist textbook market. She taught sociology through novels, short stories, and punchy essays. Gilman did speak on college and university campuses, giving guest lectures, and she wrote several nonfiction, full-length treatises, of which *Women and Economics* (1898) is the best known, but her most recognized forte was the short, surgical essay and serialized works, offered on the monthly installment plan, such as *Herland*, *With Her in Ourland*, and *The Dress of Women*. The use of fiction to teach sociological ideas to a mass, literate audience has a major precursor in the didactic novels of Harriet Martineau (Hill 1989a, 1991) and, subsequently, in the sociological novels of Mari Sandoz (Hill 1987, 1989b), thus linking Gilman to a tradition of female sociological novelists. Working largely outside the academy, Gilman sought to make sociology relevant and intelligible to the lives of everyday men and women.

Gilman wrote and published *The Forerunner* as an educational, sociological enterprise. The influence of works like *The Dress of Women*, presented over the course of a year in twelve monthly installments, was limited primarily to the regular readers of her magazine. Gilman attempted to increase readership of *The Forerunner* by offering reduced price subscriptions to the members of "Gilman Circles," envisioned as small, face-to-face groups in which the contents of each monthly issue would be discussed and debated. Sales were poor, however, and the wider audience that Gilman imagined did not materialize, thus relegating *The Dress of Women* to near total obscurity. *Herland*, however, and, more recently, *With Her in Ourland*, two novels originally published in *The Forerunner*, have been republished and have received renewed notice. Deegan (1997) argues that *Herland* and *With Her in Ourland* should properly be read as two parts of a whole, since each novel radically informs the other. Similarly, *The Dress of Women* is best read in conjunction with the two parts of Gilman's Herland/Ourland chronicle, for it systematically invokes and logically grounds the structural arguments that give rise to the utopian reveries in *Herland* and the sober critiques in *With Her in Ourland* voiced by Ellador, Gilman's peripatetic protagonist in both novels. In the same way that *Herland* and *With Her in Ourland* compliment each other, Gilman's fiction (represented here by the Herland/Ourland saga) is complimented by her nonfiction (in this case, *The Dress of Women*). Now that all three works are again readily available for reading, discussion, and critique, we commend them, *ensemble*, to would-be members of twenty-first century Gilman Circles.

Gilman, in working outside the formal academy, provides an alternative model of modern sociological practice, as did Harriet Martineau, Beatrice Webb, Jane Addams, and many other early women sociologists (Deegan 1988, 1991). Gilman engaged the wider world through writing and lecturing. She pushed, pulled, and cajoled her readers and listeners toward new understandings of the social universe and its possibilities for change and improvement.

Gilman participated in several important intellectual movements, including: cultural feminism, reform Darwinism, feminist pragmatism, Fabian socialism, and Nationalism that shared an interest in changing the economy and women's social status through social reform movements (Deegan 1997), such as the Dress Reform Movement (Gilman 1935: 234). Some of these movements were national or international in scope and organization, but their sociological nexus was concentrated in Chicago. Although not manifested in the work of many academic sociologists today, emphasis on institutional change and social reform has a long history and is rooted in the early days of American sociology. Joe R. Feagin (forthcoming), in his recent presidential address to the American Sociological Association, argues that we have much to gain by celebrating and paying attention to that history. By carefully reading Gilman's corpus, we are offered intriguing pathways for reconnecting with the exciting possibilities for change that once infused and informed sociological practice in the United States.

GILMAN AND VEBLEN: THEIR IDEAS ON WOMEN AND DRESS

Gilman and Thorstein Veblen—as contemporary sociologists, social economists, feminists, reform Darwinists, and writers who shaped the popular mind—were remarkable and powerful allies. Thorstein Bunde Veblen, born in 1857, and educated at Carleton College, Johns Hopkins, Yale, and Cornell (Johnson 1934), was three years Gilman's senior. Veblen was integral to Gilman's *The Dress of Women*, and she makes five direct references to his work. Lest today's reader judge this as thin evidence of Veblen's considerable role, it is important to note that Gilman rarely referred to other scholars and their special concepts. The fact that Gilman specifically used Veblen's concepts and identified them as such in *The Dress of Women* was highly unusual (Deegan 1997).

A significant tie between Gilman and Veblen is the latter's remarkably strong stand on women:

> Much of his work can be seen as a defense of women; Veblen regarded women as the great oppressed cadre, whether they were the slaves of marauding tribes and thus the first "private property" or the 19th-century slaves of fashion who bore the brunt of male emulation; intrinsically freer than men of such superstitions as nationalism, the women were the core carriers of social decency and simplicity under the perversions and rituals created and dominated by men. (Riesman 1953: 41)

These ideas closely mirrored those professed by Gilman.

Despite Gilman's (1935) intellectual indebtedness to many scholars, she acknowledged, in her autobiography, only a few male sociologists as friends and intellectual colleagues, namely: Lester Ward, Edward A. Ross, and Patrick Geddes (Gilman's links to these men are discussed more fully in Deegan 1997). Veblen was not named among this small circle. His influence, however, far exceeded the scattered mentions of his name in *The Dress of Women*. William Dean Howells, Gilman's friend and an important social analyst in his own right, suggested that the Gilman/Veblen relationship was one of mutual influence. Thus, he noted that Gilman wrote about women consumers in her ground-breaking *Women and Economics* in 1898, a year before Veblen (1899b) coined the concept of "conspicuous consumption" in his magnum opus, *The Theory of the Leisure Class*

(Howells, cited in Nies 1977: 144). Kathryn Sklar (1995: 403) also noted Gilman's influence, by 1899, on Veblen.

We know too that the sociologist Edward A. Ross introduced Veblen's book to Gilman early in 1900 (Gilman 1995: 342). There, Veblen presented many of his most important concepts, for example: "the leisure class," "conspicuous consumption," and "status symbols." He also discussed the problematic nature of displaying the wealth of men and families through women's adornment and leisure. In fact, in *The Theory of the Leisure Class*, Veblen (1899b) devoted an entire chapter to "Dress as an Expression of the Pecuniary Culture," an exposition that parallels Gilman's work in *The Dress of Women*. In addition, his analyses of "The Economic Theory of Women's Dress" (1894) and "The Barbarian Status of Women" (1899a) probably influenced the well-read Gilman as well.

On 27 January, 1900, Charlotte wrote her then fiance Houghton Gilman that Veblen's book exhibited "a lot of truth" (Gilman 1995: 343) and she recommended that Houghton read it. On 1 February 1900 she began work on *Concerning Children* (Gilman 1995: 343), one of her several major statements on the intersection of gender and social structure, with Veblen's ideas fresh in mind. The exact threads linking Gilman, Ross, and Veblen cannot be conclusively reconstructed on such thin evidence, but Gilman was undoubtedly reading Veblen's writing on class and work, after Ross recommended Veblen, as she continued her extensive series of books and essays on gender, labor, and society.

Gilman and Veblen had several opportunities to meet, but the record, unfortunately, does not indicate if these opportunities were realized in fact. For example, Gilman frequently lived or visited Chicago between 1895 and 1899, overlapping the period from 1892 to 1906 when Veblen lived in that midwestern metropolis (Riesman 1953: 209). Gilman and Veblen also had friends at the University of Chicago, where Veblen worked, and at Hull-House, where Gilman lived from August–November 1895, and visited frequently for extended periods between 1895 and 1899 (Deegan 1997). The probability is high that they encountered each other in Chicago and were mutually influenced, but the documentary evidence of such meetings remains undiscovered at this writing.

Textually, however, several parallels in the work of Gilman and Veblen deserve comment. In addition to Gilman's emphasis on his concept of "conspicuous consumption," she also applied the words "savage" and "barbarian" in ways similar to Veblen's usage. Both writers employed these words to refer to stages in social evolution characterized by certain institutional structures. Although these terms now have an ethnocentric, occidental ring today, both authors used these concepts as technical terms—not pejorative ones—that emerged from feminist reform Darwinism (see Deegan 1997; Nils Gilman 1999).

Both Gilman and Veblen shared another experience: both were depicted as immoral in their sexual lives. Gilman's perceived iniquities were her divorce and her joint custody of her daughter with her former husband and his new wife, one of Gilman's best friends. Veblen's perceived wickedness emerged from his reputed adulterous behavior and subsequent scandals (Nils Gilman 1999; Maynard 2000). The "immoral" reputations bestowed on Gilman and Veblen were differently gendered, but the ensuing public outrage was similar and profound in both cases. Most likely, the intensity and public nature of the scandals was rooted, in part, in their adherence to and profession of radical social ideas. In like manner, Chicago sociologist William I. Thomas, who wrote, interestingly, on "The Psychology of Women's Dress" (Thomas 1908), suffered public scandal when his alleged sexual improprieties were exploited in the nation's newspapers (Thomas 1918; Deegan 1988: 178–86). Yellow journalists depicted Gilman as a symbol of both a decadent society and the evils of feminism. Doctors, such as Gilman's physician, S. Weir Mitchell, considered women's intellectual labor a source of physical and mental decay, a situation to which Gilman (1892) responded with *The Yellow Wall-Paper* (Gilman 1892, 1913) and noted in her autobiography (Gilman 1935: 95–96, 118–21).

Yellow journalism aside, Margaret Lewis and David Sebberson (1997) persuasively argue that Gilman and Veblen share an effective rhetorical style, and that technique works against their wider academic acceptance, then and now. They were popularly admired and are still widely read today, but economists and sociologists are typically more grudging in their approval. Recently, for example, Colin Campbell (1995), sarcastically labeled Veblen's work as "conspicuous confusion" and judged his contributions as negligible. Gilman and Veblen, however, speak to a public constituency. Both Veblen and Gilman use ordinary language in their formal theories, attend to everyday economic acts and decisions, and reveal how economics shapes the ways we live. As Lewis and Sebberson (1997) put it, Gilman and Veblen resituate "economics in the world of the living for the purpose of social progress" and want to empower actors in their everyday lives. Both theorists adopt similar approaches to the act of theorizing. Comprehensive and comparative studies of their sizable and significant sets of writings are fully warranted, and—we hope—the republication of *The Dress of Women* is an instructive first step toward this larger enterprise.

CLOTH, CLOTHING, AND GENDER IN HERLAND AND OURLAND

In *The Dress of Women*, Gilman explicates the theory and critique of clothing that powers her descriptions and analyses of fashion and wearing apparel in her sociologically didactic novels, *Herland* and *With Her in Ourland*. Gilman previously discussed dress and dress-related issues (for example, Gilman 1905a, b), and in *The Dress of Women* offers a full-fledged sociological account. For Gilman, the arts of weaving and clothing construction are traditionally women's skills, skills to be honored and celebrated—as they were in the Labor Museum at Hull-House in Chicago (Washburne 1904) and in the arts and crafts movement (Deegan and Wahl, forthcoming). "Cloth," Gilman argues in the prefatory note to *The Dress of Women*, "is a social tissue," and freed from the perverse extremes occasioned by male domination of the marriage market, women's dress could be healthful, rational and highly aesthetic. Men's dress, too, can become freer, more comfortable, less starched, and more colorful. These theoretical points are given dramatic life in Gilman's handling of cloth and clothing in the Herland/Ourland narrative. In *Herland*, the men of Ourland are pointedly introduced to new ways of wearing and thinking about women's dress, and their own.

Symbolically, a piece of cloth signals the discovery of Herland by three male explorers, Vandyke Jennings, Terry Nicholson and Jeff Margrave:

> It was only a rag, a long, raveled fragment of cloth. But it was a well-woven fabric, with a pattern, and of a clear scarlet that the water had not faded. No savage tribe that we had heard of made such fabrics.

The high quality of the fabric implies an advanced state of civilization:

> "There is no such cloth made by any of these local tribes," I announced, examining those rags with great care. "Somewhere up yonder they spin and weave and dye—as well as we do."

"That would mean a considerable civilization, Van. There couldn't be such a place—and not known about."

But, in the men's minds, the production of fabric, while fundamental to civilization, also marks the rudimentary limit of civilized accomplishment, beyond which women may strive but not succeed:

". . . we mustn't look for inventions and progress; it'll be awfully primitive."

"How about that cloth mill?" Jeff suggested.

"Oh, cloth! Women have always been spinsters. But there they stop—you'll see."

As the three men enter Herland, they look to dress, as they have been socialized, for gender clues:

We had all seen babies, children big and little, everywhere that we had come near enough to distinguish the people. And though by dress we could not be sure of all the grown persons, still there had not been one man that we were certain of.

And, on first meeting a few representatives of Herland, the men discover that glittering gifts of adornment, calculated to beguile the women of Ourland, lack the desired effect in Herland. The tokens are simply acknowledged, no woman swoons in appreciation:

[Terry] stepped forward, with his brilliant ingratiating smile, and made low obeisance to the women before him. Then he produced another tribute, a broad soft scarf of filmy texture, rich in color and pattern, a lovely thing, even to my eye, and offered it with a deep bow to the tall unsmiling woman who seemed to head the ranks before him. She took it with a gracious nod of acknowledgment, and passed it on to those behind her.

He tried again, this time bringing out a circlet of rhinestones, a glittering crown that should have pleased any woman on earth. He made a brief address, including Jeff and me as partners in his enterprise, and with another bow presented this. Again his gift was accepted and, as before, passed out of sight.

The men soon realize that they have stumbled into a world discernably populated only by women: "They're all women, in spite of their nondescript clothes . . . ," a world wherein gender and clothing are subject to new rules. Early on, the reader of *Herland* learns that cloth, clothing, and adornment, and the social rules that govern their use in Herland are not what we are accustomed to in Ourland, in the real world. And when the men initially resist the discipline of Herland, they are subdued not by guns, knives, or spears, but by a moist anesthetic administered by "a firm hand holding a wetted cloth before mouth and nose." A piece of cloth leads the men to Herland, which they initially underestimate, and now a piece of cloth becomes the instrument of their capture.

The Herland environment—of which clothing and fabrics are integral parts—is rational, comfortable, and meets the highest aesthetic standards. Van reports, on awakening from the anesthesia:

> The most prominent sensation was of absolute physical comfort. I was lying in a perfect bed: long, broad, smooth; firmly soft and level; with the finest linen, some warm light quilt of blanket, and a counterpane that was a joy to the eye.

The men's clothing was replaced by Herland garments:

> Terry swung his legs out of bed, stood up, stretched himself mightily. He was in a long nightrobe, a sort of seamless garment, undoubtedly comfortable—we all found ourselves so covered. Shoes were beside each bed, also quite comfortable and good looking though by no means like our own. . . . Then we made a search of the big room again and found a large airy closet, holding plenty of clothing, but not ours.

The men, however, adapt appreciatively to the new clothing:

> "No use kicking, boys," I said. "They've got us, and apparently they're perfectly harmless. It remains for us to cook up some plan of escape like any other bottled heroes. Meanwhile we've got to put on these clothes—Hobson's choice."
>
> The garments were simple in the extreme, and absolutely comfortable, physically, though of course we all felt like supes in the theater. There was a one-piece cotton undergarment, thin and soft, that reached over the knees and shoulders, something like the one-piece pajamas some fellows wear, and a kind of half-hose, that came up to just under the knee and stayed there—had elastic tops of their own, and covered the edges of the first.
>
> Then there was a thicker variety of union suit, a lot of them in the closet, of varying weights and somewhat sturdier material—evidently they would do at a pinch with nothing further. Then there were tunics, knee-length, and some long robes. Needless to say, we took tunics.

We bathed and dressed quite cheerfully.

"Not half bad," said Terry, surveying himself in a long mirror. His hair was somewhat longer than when we left the last barber, and the hats provided were much like those seen on the prince in the fairy tale, lacking the plume.

The costume was similar to that which we had seen on all the women, though some of them, those working in the fields, glimpsed by our glasses when we first flew over, wore only the first two.

I settled my shoulders and stretched my arms, remarking: "They have worked out a mighty sensible dress, I'll say that for them." With which we all agreed.

They further discover the practicality of Herland dress:

We were free to study as much as we wished, and were not left merely to wander in the garden for recreation but introduced to a great gymnasium. ... No change of costume was needed for this work, save to lay off outer clothing. The first one was as perfect a garment for exercise as need be devised, absolutely free to move in, and, I had to admit, much better-looking than our usual one.

Dress, per se, ceases to distinguish gender: "So there we sat, at ease; all in similar dress; our hair, by now, as long as theirs, only our beards to distinguish us," allowing the men to appreciate the inherent qualities of Herland's clothing, as clothing, freed from the gendered social functions of clothing in Ourland:

We had become well used to the clothes. They were quite as comfortable as our own—in some ways more so—and undeniably better looking. As to pockets, they left nothing to be desired. That second garment was fairly quilted with pockets. They were most ingeniously arranged, so as to be convenient to the hand and not inconvenient to the body, and were so placed as at once to strengthen the garment and add decorative lines of stitching.

In this, as in so many other points we had now to observe, there was shown the action of a practical intelligence, coupled with fine artistic feeling, and, apparently, untrammeled by any injurious influences.

Gilman holds that in nature, the male of each species is almost always the most colorful, and in *Herland*, her three male protagonists, given the chance, demonstrate this trait:

I remember ... how careful we were about our clothes, and our amateur barbering. Terry, in particular, was fussy to a degree about the cut of his beard, and so critical of our combined efforts, that we handed him the shears and told him to please himself. We began to rather prize those beards of ours; they were almost our sole distinction among those tall and sturdy women, with their cropped hair and sexless costume. Being offered a wide selection of garments, we had chosen according to our personal taste, and were surprised to find, on meeting large audiences, that we were the most highly decorated, especially Terry.

He was a very impressive figure, his strong features softened by the somewhat longer hair—though he made me trim it as closely as I knew how; and he wore his richly embroidered tunic with its broad, loose girdle with quite a Henry V air. Jeff looked more like—well, like a Huguenot Lover; and I don't know what I looked like, only that I felt very comfortable. When I got back to our own padded armor and its starched borders I realized with acute regret how comfortable were those Herland clothes.

With the balance of nature restored, with men as the peacocks, rather than the dull reverse, the three explorers are enabled to *see* the women of Herland, undistracted by the peculiarities of "sexy" dressing so common in Ourland:

The thing that Terry had so complained of when we first came—that they weren't "feminine," they lacked "charm," now became a great comfort. Their vigorous beauty was an aesthetic pleasure, not an irritant. Their dress and ornaments had not a touch of the "come-and-find-me" element.

There are no women dressing to "please" or "catch" men in Herland, but Ourland brims over with examples of perverse dress practices.

In *With Her in Ourland: Sequel to Herland*, Gilman draws direct connections between the subordinate status of women and the clothes they wear. Vandyke Jennings now tours Ourland, the real world, with his new wife, Ellador, a resident of Herland. In chapter eleven, Ellador addresses the status of "kept" women, and drives home her point by asking Van to ponder the image of men dressed in women's "sexy" clothing:

"Put yourself in my place for a moment, Van. Suppose in Herland we had a lot of—subject men. Blame us all you want to for doing it, but look at the men. Little creatures, undersized and generally feeble. Cowardly and not ashamed of it. Kept for sex purposes only or as servants; or both, usually both. I confess I'm asking something difficult of your imagination, but try to think of Herland women, each with a soft man she kept to cook for her, to wait upon her and to—'love' when she pleased. Ignorant men mostly. Poor men, almost all, having to ask their owners for money and tell what they wanted it for. Some of them utterly degraded creatures, kept in houses for common use—as women are kept here. Some of them quite gay and happy—pet men, with pet names and presents showered upon them. Most of them contented, piously accepting kitchen work as their duty, living by the religion and laws and customs the women made. Some of them left out and made fun of for being left—not owned at all—and envying those who were! Allow for a surprising percentage of mutual love and happiness, even under these conditions; but also for ghastly depths of misery and a general low level of mere submission to the inevitable. Then in this state of degradation fancy these men for the most part quite content to make monkeys of themselves by wearing the most ridiculous clothes. Fancy them, men, with men's bodies, though enfeebled, wearing open-work lace underclothing, with little ribbons all strung through it; wearing dresses never twice alike and almost always foolish; wearing hats—" she fixed me with a steady eye in which a growing laughter twinkled—"wearing such hats as your women wear!"

Gilman's point is not that cross-dressing is absurd, but that dressing in ridiculous clothing—male or female—is preposterous.

Women's fashions, in Gilman's view, were becoming ever more extreme, despite the women's movement. Ellador asks, and Van responds:

". . . I suppose women used to dress more foolishly than they do now. Can that be possible?"

I ran over in my mind some of the eccentricities of fashion in earlier periods and was about to say that it was possible when I chanced to look out of the window. It was a hot day, most oppressively hot, with a fiercely glaring sun. A woman stood just across the street talking to a man. I picked up my opera glass and studied her for a moment. I had read that "the small waist is coming in again." Hers had come. She stood awkwardly in extremely high-heeled slippers, in which the sole of the foot leaned on a steep slant from heel to ball, and her toes, poor things, were driven into the narrow-pointed toe of the slipper by the whole sliding weight of the body above. The thin silk hose showed the insteps puffing up like a pincushion from the binding grip of that short vamp.

Her skirts were short as a child's, most voluminous and varied in outline, hanging in bunches on the hips and in various fluctuating points and corners below. The bodice was a particolored composition, of indiscreet exposures, more suitable for a ballroom than for the street.

But what struck me most was that she wore about her neck a dead fox or the whole outside of one.

No, she was not a lunatic. No, that man was not her keeper. No, it was not a punishment, not an initiation penalty, not an election bet.

That woman, of her own free will and at considerable expense, wore heavy furs in the hottest summer weather.

I laid down the glass and turned to Ellador. "No, my dear," said I gloomily. "It is not possible that women ever could have been more idiotic in dress than that."

Ever the optimist, however, Gilman believed that Ourland, the real world, can be salvaged, and if not all at once, we can at least begin with the clothing in which we live and work. Undoubtedly, a more "relaxed" attitude toward clothing is evident today, especially on college campuses, than was true in Gilman's day, but the underlying pervasiveness of gender display through dress is still everywhere in evidence—and it is to this fundamental, structural issue that Gilman speaks directly and persuasively in *The Dress of Women*.

Finally, a note on the editing and preparation of this edition. We append, in several notes, identifications of many of Gilman's referents and sources. We correct several obvious typographical/typesetting errors appearing in the 1915 serialized version of *The Dress of Women*. We also standardize spellings in those few places where the effect is unobtrusive and contributes to readability and consistency. The more peculiar time-bound spellings of Gilman's era, however, and her sometimes inventive (e.g., "divigation") and sometimes archaic word choices (e.g., "caddice worms"), we always allow to stand. All of the ellipses, dashes, and strings of asterisks found in our edition are reproduced, to the best of our ability, exactly as they stood in *The Forerunner*. In no case does an ellipsis or other similar device indicate that we deleted anything from Gilman's text. We again acknowledge having added the subtitle: *A Critical Introduction to the Symbolism and Sociology of Clothing*, as we believe it underscores Gilman's intent and will usefully assist those of our colleagues and students who rely increasingly on keyword-guided bibliographic searches to discover Gilman's remarkable sociological work. With the insight that the publication of *The Dress of Women* provides, we look forward to future, expanded understandings of Gilman's work on clothing, self, and gender.

REFERENCES

Campbell, Colin. 1995. "Conspicuous Confusion? A Critique of Veblen's Theory of Conspicuous Consumption." *Sociological Theory* 13 (March): 37–47.

Deegan, Mary Jo. 1981. "Early Women Sociologists and the American Sociological Society: Patterns of Exclusion and Participation." *American Sociologist* 16 (February): 14–24.

———. 1987. "An American Dream: The Historical Connections between Women, Humanism, and Sociology, 1890–1920." *Humanity and Society* 11 (August): 353–65.

———. 1988. *Jane Addams and the Men of the Chicago School, 1892–1918*. New Brunswick, NJ: Transaction.

———, ed. 1991. *Women in Sociology: A Bio-bibliographical Sourcebook*. Westport, CT: Greenwood Press.

———. 1997. "Gilman's Sociological Journey from *Herland* to *Ourland*." Pp. 1–57 in *With Her in Ourland: Sequel to Herland*, by Charlotte Perkins Gilman, edited by Mary Jo Deegan and Michael R. Hill. Westport, CT: Greenwood Press.

Deegan, Mary Jo, and Christopher W. Podeschi. Forthcoming. "The Ecofeminist Pragmatism of Charlotte Perkins Gilman." *Environmental Ethics*.

Deegan, Mary Jo, and Ana-Maria Wahl. Forthcoming. "Arts and Crafts in Chicago and Britain: The Sociology of Ellen Gates Starr at Hull-House." In *Windows and Mirrors: Essays in the History of Sociology*, edited by Janusz Mucha, Wlodzimierz Winclawski, and Dirk Käsler. Toruń (Poland): Nicholas Copernicus University Press.

Degler, Carl N. 1956. "Charlotte Perkins Gilman on the Theory and Practice of Feminism." Pp. 11–29 in *Charlotte Perkins Gilman: The Woman and Her Work*, edited by Sheryl L. Meyering. Ann Arbor, MI: UMI Research Press, 1989.

———. 1966. "Introduction." Pp. vi–xxxv in *Women and Economics: A Study of the Economic Relations between Men and Women as a Factor in Social Evolution*, by Charlotte Perkins Gilman, edited by Carl N. Degler. New York: Harper and Row.

Feagin, Joe R. Forthcoming. "Social Justice and Sociology: Agendas for the 21st Century." *American Sociological Review*.

Gilman, Charlotte Perkins. 1892. *The Yellow Wall-Paper*, with an afterword by Elaine Hedges. Old Westbury, NY: Feminist Press, 1973.

———. 1898. *Women and Economics*. Boston: Small and Maynard.

———. 1905a. "Symbolism in Dress." *The Independent* 58 (8 June): 1294–97.

———. 1905b. "Why These Clothes?" *The Independent* 58 (2 March): 466–69.

———. 1907a. "Social Consciousness." *American Journal of Sociology* 12 (March): 690–91.

———. 1907b. "Social Darwinism." *American Journal of Sociology* 12 (March): 713–14.

———. 1908. "Suggestion of the Negro Problem." *American Journal of Sociology* 14 (July): 178–85.

———. 1909. "How Home Conditions React Upon the Family." *American Journal of Sociology* 14 (March): 592–605.

———. 1913. "Why I Wrote the Yellow Wallpaper." *The Forerunner* 4 (October): 27.

———. 1915. *Herland, The Yellow Wall-paper, and Selected Readings*, edited by Denise D. Knight. New York: Penguin, 1999.

———. 1916. *With Her in Ourland: Sequel to Herland*, edited by Mary Jo Deegan and Michael R. Hill. Westport, CT: Greenwood, 1997.

———. 1935. *The Living of Charlotte Perkins Gilman: An Autobiography*. Madison, WI: University of Wisconsin Press, 1990.

———. 1994. *The Diaries of Charlotte Perkins Gilman*, edited by Denise D. Knight. 2 vols. Charlottesville, VA: University Press of Virginia.

———. 1995. *A Journey from Within: The Love Letters of Charlotte Perkins Gilman, 1897–1900*, edited by Mary A. Hill. Lewisburg, PA: Bucknell University Press.

———. 1998. *The Abridged Diaries of Charlotte Perkins Gilman*, edited by Denise D. Knight. Charlottesville: University Press of Virginia.

Gilman, Nils. 1999. "Thorstein Veblen's Neglected Feminism." *Journal of Economic Issues* 33 (September): 689–712.

Goffman, Erving. 1959. *The Presentation of Self in Everyday Life*. Garden City, NY: Doubleday.

———. 1979. *Gender Advertisements*. Cambridge, MA: Harvard University Press.

Golden, Catherine, and Joanna S. Zangrando, eds. 2000. *The Mixed Legacy of Charlotte Perkins Gilman*. Newark: University of Delaware Press.

Hill, Mary A. 1980. *Charlotte Perkins Gilman: The Making of a Radical Feminist, 1860–1896*. Philadelphia, PA: Temple University Press.

Hill, Michael R. 1987. "Novels, Thought Experiments, and Humanist Sociology in the Classroom: Mari Sandoz and *Capital City*." *Teaching Sociology* 15: 38–44.

———. 1989a. "Empiricism and Reason in Harriet Martineau's Sociology." Pp. xv–lx in *How to Observe Morals and Manners*, by Harriet Martineau. Sesquicentennial edition. New Brunswick, NJ: Transaction Books.

———. 1989b. "Mari Sandoz' Sociological Imagination: *Capital City* as an Ideal Type." *Platte Valley Review* 17 (1): 102–22.

———. 1991. "Harriet Martineau." Pp. 289–97 in *Women in Sociology: A Bio-*

bibliographical Sourcebook, edited by Mary Jo Deegan. Westport, CT: Greenwood Press.

———. 1996. "Herland." Pp. 251–54 in *Masterpieces of Women's Literature*, edited by Frank N. Magill. New York: HarperCollins.

Johnson, Alvin. 1934. "Veblen, Thorstein Bunde (1857–1929)." Pp. 234–35 in *Encyclopaedia of the Social Sciences*, Vol. 15, edited by E.R.A. Seligman and Alvin Johnson. New York: Macmillan.

Karpinski, Joanne B., ed. 1992. *Critical Essays on Charlotte Perkins Gilman*. New York: G.K. Hall.

Keith, Bruce. 1991. "Charlotte Perkins Gilman." Pp. 148–56 in *Women in Sociology: A Bio-bibliographical Sourcebook*, edited by Mary Jo Deegan. Westport, CT: Greenwood Press.

Kessler, Carol Farley. 1995. *Charlotte Perkins Gilman: Her Progress toward Utopia with Selected Writings*. Syracuse, NY: Syracuse University Press.

Knight, Denise D. 1997. *Charlotte Perkins Gilman: A Study of the Short Fiction*. New York: Twayne.

———. 1999. "Introduction." Pp. ix–xxiv in *Herland, the Yellow Wall-Paper, and Selected Writings*, by Charlotte Perkins Gilman, edited by Denise D. Knight. New York: Penguin.

Lane, Ann J. 1990. *To Herland and Beyond: The Life and Work of Charlotte Perkins Gilman*. New York: Pantheon.

Lemert, Charles C., 1997. *Social Things: An Introduction to the Sociological Life*. Lanham, MD: Rowman & Littlefield.

Lengermann, Patricia Madoo, and Jill Niebrugge-Brantley. 1998. *The Women Founders: Sociology and Social Theory, 1830–1930: A Text/Reader*. Boston, MA: McGraw-Hill.

Lewis, Margaret, and David Sebberson. 1997. "The Rhetoricality of Economic Theory: Charlotte Perkins Gilman and Thorstein Veblen." *Journal of Economic Issues* 31 (June): 417–24.

Magner, Lois N. 1978. "Women and the Scientific Idiom: Textual Episodes from Wollstonecraft, Fuller, Gilman, and Firestone." *Signs: Journal of Women in Culture and Society* 4 (Autumn): 61–80.

Mayering, Sheryl L., ed. 1989. *Charlotte Perkins Gilman: The Woman and Her Work*. Ann Arbor, MI: UMI Research Press.

Maynard, Tony. 2000. "A Shameless Lothario: Thorstein Veblen as Sexual Predator and Sexual Liberator." *Journal of Economic Issues* 34 (March): 194–201.

Nies, Judith. 1977. *Seven Women: Portraits from the American Radical Tradition*. New York: Viking Press.

O'Neill, William L. 1967. *Divorce in the Progressive Era*. New York: New Viewpoints.

———. 1972. "Introduction." Pp. vii–xvii in *The Home: Its Work and Influ-*

ences, by Charlotte Perkins Gilman. Urbana, IL: University of Illinois Press.

Riesman, David. 1953. *Thorstein Veblen: A Critical Interpretation*. New York: Charles Scribners.

Rossi, Alice., ed. 1973. *The Feminist Papers*. New York: Columbia University Press.

Rudd, Jill, and Val Gough. 1999. *Charlotte Perkins Gilman: Optimist Reformer*. Iowa City, IA: University of Iowa Press.

Scharnhost, Gary. 1985a. *Charlotte Perkins Gilman*. Boston, MA: Twayne.

———. 1985b. *Charlotte Perkins Gilman: A Bibliography*. Metuchen, NJ: Scarecrow.

Sinclair, Andrew. 1966. *The Emancipation of the American Woman*. New York: Harper and Row.

Sklar, Kathryn Kish. 1995. *Florence Kelley and the Nation's Work*. New Haven, CT: Yale University Press.

Stetson, Charles Walter. 1985. *Endure: The Diaries of Charles Walter Stetson*, edited by Mary A. Hill. Philadelphia, PA: Temple University Press.

Sydie, R. A., and Bert Adams. Forthcoming. "Beatrice Webb and Charlotte Perkins Gilman: Feminist Debates and Contradictions." *Sociological Origins* 2 (1).

Terry, James L. 1983. "Bringing Women . . . In: A Modest Proposal." *Teaching Sociology* 10 (January): 251–61.

Thomas, William I. 1908. "The Psychology of Women's Dress." *American Magazine* 67 (November): 66–72.

———. 1918. "Thomas Defends Self as a Daring Social Explorer." *Chicago Tribune* (22 April): 16ff.

Veblen, Thorstein. 1894. "The Economic Theory of Women's Dress." *Popular Science Monthly* 46 (December): 198–205.

———. 1899a. "The Barbarian Status of Women." *American Journal of Sociology* 4 (January): 503–14.

———. 1899b. *The Theory of the Leisure Class: An Economic Study of Institutions*. New York: Macmillan.

Washburne, Marion Foster. 1904. "A Labor Museum." *The Craftsman* 6 (September): 570–80.

The Dress of Women

Prefatory Note

CLOTH is a social tissue.

By means of its convenient sheathing we move among one another freely, smoothly, and in peace, when without it such association would be impossible. The more solitary we live, the less we think of clothing; the more we crowd and mingle in "society," the more we think of it.

The evolution of textile manufacture is as long and interesting as any chapter of our social growth.

From braided hair, perhaps, or thongs, to the plaiting of reeds and grasses and stripped bark, up to the fine tissues of cotton and flax, wool and silk; from the coarse accidental felt of matted camel's hair to the finest of laces; it is as vivid a picture of natural growth as human life can show.

Other creatures grow their clothing on their individual bodies; scales, or bristles, fur or feathers—they have but one suit, self-replenished. They may clean it perhaps, but cannot change it—save indeed for the seasonal changes, the difference between youth and age, and—the chameleon.

The human animal shows in its clothing as conspicuously as in many other ways, the peculiar power of extra-physical expression.

As by his tools and weapons he surpasses in varied efficiency the perhaps more perfect, but limited, mechanism of any other creature; so in clothing he is enabled to adapt himself to conditions more rapidly than by moulting or casting the skin; and from this basic advantage goes on to a widening range of uses even yet scarcely appreciated.

Our clothing is as literally evolved to meet our needs as the scales of a fish or the feathers of a bird. It grows on us, socially, as theirs grow on them individually.

Because we manufacture a substance, consciously and through a number of hands and brains, it is none the less a natural product of society.

Because a substance or implement does not physiologically grow on us, it may be nevertheless an integral part of the social tissues; and, equally may be a superfluous, a detrimental part, or a positive disease and danger.

Clothing studied in this way, is a sort of social skin, adapting itself to conditions of heat and cold as do the coverings of other animals, only more quickly. If the polar bear in our menageries could take off his underflannels; or if the equatorial monkeys could put them on—they would suffer somewhat less.

But our clothing, through its changeability and its variety, has become, even more than is an epidermis, a medium of expression. The most our skin can do, to show emotion, is to blush, to pale, to contract so that the hair rises; but with clothing we may express a whole gamut of emotions from personal vanity to class consciousness.

In our various fabrics we have created something without parallel in nature. The nearest to it is, of course, the animal integuments. As a manufactured article the web of a spider comes nearest perhaps, or the nest-building material of some birds and insects.

A smooth, soft, continuous substance, of equal thinness and flexibility throughout, cloth itself fluttering in the breeze as flags do, or hanging in rich folds of drapery, is an addition to the beauty of the world.

When those soft folds, those rippling undulations, are added to the grace and action of the human body, we have a new element of beauty, recognized by sculptors and painters of all time.

. . . .

To follow the industrial evolution of textiles would be a great work in itself, not here attempted. Similarly to study the evolution of costume is another great work, of which but the nearest sketch of a skeleton is given here.

As a natural phenomenon, subject to natural laws of development under all our arbitrary modifications, it is interesting to note the few and simple seeds from which have grown the mighty efflorescence of our coverings.

For warmth the shivering savage wraps the skin of his victim around him. To keep it on he cuts a hole for his head. To hold it close he ties a thong around it.

Here is the origin of the first Garment, the tunic, or shirt, still in constant use.

As ingenuity increased the loose folds were sewed together and the surplus cut out. When cloth was woven in long strips the simpler straight-down shape naturally developed.

With or without sleeves, loose or fitted, long or short, this is the parent of most of the clothing of humanity.

It may be abbreviated to the scantest undershirt, or trail for yards on the floor as a voluminous robe—its ancestry is one.

The skirt is but the lower half cut loose from the upper; the "petticoat," as the name implies, once but a smaller undergarment otherwise similar to the outer coat; jacket and jerkin have but the distinction of being open in front and varying in length; every garment that goes over the head, or is put on arms first, is descended from the primitive tunic.

From the lower extremities come the rest of our garments.

First the sandal for protection, the moccasin for warmth, the upward elongating "leggings," which appear at length as trousers; every variety of shoe and stocking, boot and garter, foot and leg-wear of all sorts, grew from those small beginnings.

Things to be dropped from above and hang down; things to be lifted from below and fastened up; these are the two main lines of evolution in garments.

This much is easy to hold in mind, and also the main influences affecting the development, such as climate, or methods of industry.

The trousered races seemed to begin in colder countries; bare legs are not comfortable in snow. Yet trousers linger, turned to muslin, when northern races invade and remain in more southern lands.

When studying in more detail certain articles of dress, or tendencies, the evolutionary process comes in as reference, but it is not the principal part of the subject as here considered.

This study treats in the main of the relation between dress and women; in different races, in different classes, in different periods, and particularly in regard to the present status of modern women, and the hastening changes in that status now so evident.

[Charlotte Perkins Gilman]

Chapter One

Primary Motives in Clothing

THE MOTIVES which underlie the wide variations of human costume are reducible to a few main lines of causation.

We may define these five, not as absolutely exclusive, but as roughly accounting for the majority of phenomena in clothing:

a. Protection.
b. Warmth.
c. Decoration.
d. Modesty.
e. Symbolism.

These may at times overlap, but there is a clear distinction, even between the first two. The five are arranged in their order of appearance.

The very first article put on and worn by human kind, for long the only one, is that so feelingly described by Kipling in "Gunga Din."[1]

> "The garment that 'e wore
> Was nothin' much before,
> And a little less than 'arf o' that be'ind"—

namely the breechclout. This is worn purely for protective purposes, not for warmth or decoration, and long before modesty was thought of.

So the sandal and shoe originated from the same need—to protect the foot from injury—and so the hat, in its remote beginnings, was really intended to protect the head.

Among women the coverings for head and feet had this same origin, little as one would think so now; and as a purely protective appliance some form of stay or breast girdle early proved its usefulness.

This mechanical influence in dress may be traced all up the line of growth, often obscured and sometimes contradicted by the other modifying forces, but always discoverable.

The leather-patched riding-breeches, the driver's gloves, the fisherman's hip-boots, the farmer's wide-brimmed straw hat, the rubber overshoes, the motor-veil or goggles—these are evolved for protective purposes.

Closely allied to this motive is that of warmth; garments of wool and fur being devised as a "protection" against cold. But the distinction is seen in those examples used in hot countries and existing long before man had succeeded in facing northern climates.

The need of warmth, as a modifying influence in clothing, is one of the greatest. It might be hastily called the greatest if we were not familiar with developments of costume in the southern countries; or if we failed to understand the influence of the last three motives—decoration, modesty, symbolism.

The direct use of dressed hides with the fur on is still the mainstay of arctic or antarctic peoples. The Russian mujik's sheepskin, or the shaggy "chaps" of the cowboy, meet the same need in the same way as the Eskimo "paki"—they retain bodily heat.

Mackinaw coat, Jaeger underwear; flannel petticoat (a vanished rudiment with many women today)—there is a vast array of clothing based on this single necessity of keeping warm.

In temperate climates we "moult" our flannels in the Spring, and put on thicker coats in the Fall just as the animals do—though with more trouble and expense.

In these first two, and in part of the next—Decoration, we do by manufacture what other creatures do by growth. Beyond these our human coverings show new forces at work.

The animal develops callosities, as of the camel's knees; cushions of thick hair or horny pads for the feet; water-proofing for feathers, and other protective appliances; and for warmth he does just what we do—puts on a covering—grows it, to be sure, but grows it for that purpose.

In decoration he sets us a splendid example. "He" is used here not only in our usual incorrect androcentric sense, as representing the race, but most correctly as representing that part of the race essentially given to decoration.

The earliest development in decoration is unquestionably along sex lines, and is peculiarly masculine.

Among some insects such as butterflies, whose brief winged career is for the mating period, this decorative effect appears in both sexes, though even here the male leads for the most part; but speaking generally of animal life, the "decorative appendages" appear exclusively upon the male.

We are quite familiar with this fact as instanced by birds. It is the cock of all sorts, from the combed and wattled barnyard rooster to the bird of paradise, ostrich, turkey-cock or peacock; it is always the male who struts and spreads his impressive tail feathers, raises his crest and flaps his showy wings.

Decoration in human clothing follows two distinct lines; the earlier one of display for motives of sex-attraction, and the later one of that higher beauty sense in us, which delights in color, in form, in design, for an aesthetic pleasure, quite disconnected from the first.

A child's delight in new shoes, or the preference of one of us for a given color, or for a special fabric, is not based on sex-attraction. A broad and discriminating study might be made here, with some history of costume as a base, taking up garment after garment, period after period, and showing, in the decorative quality of a given article of dress just how much is due to the sex-impulse and how much to a later, purely human aesthetic sense.

Where we find certain fabrics, shapes or colors used mainly in the mating season—youth, and preferred neither in childhood or in age; especially where such choices are made by men, or by women intending to attract men, such decorative effects may be attributed to the sex impulse; but where choices are made on grounds of personal taste lasting through life, or changing with our growth to higher perceptions, we may trace them to the beauty sense of humanity.

Take the primitive and intensely personal decoration of tattooing, carried to a high point of intricacy and precision in certain tribes. There may be special patterns and distinctions as between men and women, but both sexes admire that delicate tracery of design as we admire lace or embroidery, or as we admire similar ornamentation on pottery, tools or furniture.

The primal laws of design and our pleasure in them reach deeper and higher than sex. From simple repetition and alternation, on through symmetry, radiation, and the rest, we respond to regularity, to balance, to the lifting and soothing effect of line, form, color, having no connection whatever with sex or sex-attraction.

For the male bird to manifest lovely plumes, for the male baboon to manifest unlovely callosities, for the young man to burst forth in glowing neckties, for the young woman to prink and preen for his allurement—all this is sex-decoration, but the beadwork put on her baby's wrappings by the patient squaw, or on her close-woven basketry, is decoration, to be sure, but not of sex.

We shall see later how these two distinct influences contradict one another often in our human dress, and especially in the dress of women.

Modesty, as the word is commonly understood, is a distinctly human invention.

There is the modesty which is allied to humility, as of youth, of inexperience, of comparative knowledge (I was about to say "of comparative ignorance," but ignorance is not modest; real knowledge is), but this is not what we mean in our common use of the word.

We mean by modesty a form of sex-consciousness, especially peculiar to woman. For a maiden to blush and cast down her eyes when a man approaches her is an instance of this "modesty." It shows that she knows he is a male and she is a female, and her manner calls attention to the fact. If she met him clear-eyed and indifferent, as if she was a boy, or he was a woman, this serene indifference is not at all "modest."

So "modesty" in dress, as applied to that of women, consists in giving the most conspicuous prominence of femininity.

The mere insistence on a totally different costume for men and women is based on this idea—that we should never forget sex.

A most variable thing is this modesty. It is one of the innumerable proofs of our peculiar psychic power to attach emotions to objects without the faintest shadow of real connection.

We showed this power in earliest savagery in our rich profusion of signs and omens. Fear, hope, anger, discouragement, were arbitrarily attached to bird, beast or falling leaf—to wind, cloud or water—anything would do. Like those cumbrous "memory systems" where you learn to remember a thing by first remembering another thing, we filled our mental world with arbitrary associations. This was "sacred," "holy"; this was "tabu," and this, "anathema."

So in regard to the human body, its functions and its clothing, we have obscured the simple truths of nature by a thousand extravagant notions of our own.

The clothing of men is most modified by physical conditions.

The clothing of women is most modified by psychic conditions. As they were restricted to a very limited field of activity, and as their personal comfort was of no importance to anyone, it was possible to maintain in their dress the influence of primitive conditions long outgrown by men.

And as, while men have varied widely in the manifold relations of our later economic and political growth, women have remained for the most part all in one relation—that of sex; we see at once why the dress of men has developed along lines of practical efficiency and general human distinction, while the dress of women is still most modified by the various phases of sex-distinction.

A man may run in our streets, or row, visibly, on our rivers, in a costume—a lack of costume—which for women would be called grossly immodest. He may bathe, publicly, and in company with women, so nearly naked as to shock even himself, sometimes; while the women beside him are covered far more fully than in evening dress.

Why it should be "modest" for a woman to exhibit neck, arms and shoulders, back and bosom, and immodest to go bathing without stockings, no one so much as attempts to explain.

We have attached sentiments of modesty to certain parts of the human frame and not to others—that is all.

The parts vary. There are African damsels, I have read, who will snatch off the last garment to hide their faces withal. The Breton peasant woman must cover her hair, to show it is an indecency.

We need not look for a reason where there never was one. These distinctions sprang from emotion or mere caprice, and vary with them.

But whatever our notions of modesty in dress may be, we apply them to women for the most part and not to men.

The next great governing influence in dress is Symbolism.

We do not commonly realize how strong is this influence in modifying our attire.

Even in the more directly practical garments of men, the symbolic element cries loudly, though unnoticed.

See, in instance, that badge of dignity, the "top hat." Since the days of the Pharaohs, and earlier, men have sought to express a towering sense of personal dignity by tall head-gear. The bishop's mitre, the lofty triple crown of the Pope, the high black head-gear of ancient wiseacres—these and more form instances of this quite natural effort to loom large in the eyes of lower folk.

No rounded head-fitting cap, no broad-brimmed shelter, gives that air of majesty, the truly noble head-cover must stand high.

In simple early times rude warriors wore horns on their heads, and other fear-inspiring decorations. In old Japan fearsome masks were supposed to awe the enemy. As this direct attempt was outgrown the subtler symbolic forms appeared, and crested helms bristled above the fierce-eyed fighters, just as the stiffened hairs of fighting beasts rise above their red visages.

The whole field of military uniforms shows us more symbolism than use. Only now are we beginning to wear the plain, inconspicuous khaki, or dull grey, since concealment has been expensively proved to be more profitable than ostentation. Our soldiers now are clothed in a "protective mimicry" worthy of nature's best efforts.

One modern necessity of gentlemen's dress which rests on symbolism alone is starch. The workman, warm, perspiring, delving in dirt, eschews starch. His toiling wife has labor enough to make his shirts clean, let alone "doing them up."

But he of wealth and leisure, or one whose occupation allows him to imitate the aspect of wealth and leisure, shines in starch.

Starch is not beautiful. To clothe a human figure, or any part of it, in a stiff glittering white substance, is in direct contradiction to the lines and action of the body. One might as well hang a dinner-plate across his chest, as the glaring frontlet so beloved of the masculine heart.

Starch is not comfortable, not even when the supporting integument is smooth and whole, and when worn to a raw edge, then starch becomes an instrument of moderate torture.

Starch is not cleanness. Soap, warm water, rubbing, boiling, rinsing—these remove the dirt from our clothing and leave it clean, as the sunlight bleaches it. To smooth the wrinkled surface with a hot iron makes undergarments feel better and any garment look better. But to take a cleaned article and soak it in paste, afterwards polishing it as we do our shoes, does not add to its cleanness.

Besides, starch is worn in a conspicuous exterior position, for show. No gentleman gladdens his soul by starched underwear. And those most anxious to look clean, that is, to present unbroken glittering starch to view, change the outer shirt oftener than the under shirt—which needs it most.

In Veblen's illuminating book, *The Theory of the Leisure Class*, he shows how much of what is done by the rich is done merely to exhibit their riches—in pure symbolism.[2] Either in "conspicuous leisure" or "conspicuous waste," they seek to blazon forth the fact that they do not have to work, and that they are abundantly able to pay.

The Chinese Mandarin's prolonged finger-nails—growing to such a length that he must needs wear the slender "nail-case" to protect them, are pure symbolism. No man who did anything with his hands could possibly have such nails. They furnish visible proof of the complete incapacity of such hands.

We are not so extreme in our contempt for hand labor, but the display of pink and pointed nails is found among those who neither sew, wash dishes nor tend the baby.

So our starched linen, while not extreme enough to prevent all action, finds its main value in proving that the wearer is not "a working man"—at least not a hand-worker—and that he is able to pay for the useless labor of stiffening and polishing his linen.

The element of symbolism is interwoven with even such a practical garment as the trousers. The small boy's mad desire to get into his first trousers is not based on added comfort or freedom, but on the proud exhibition of the fact that he is a boy.

Some mothers, meekly accepting the ignominy attached to their sex and therefore to their garments, dress a little boy in petticoats—for a punishment.

Yet in countries where women wear trousers and men skirts, the same sentiments would doubtless be aroused by the exactly opposite garments. These feelings are purely associate, and are attached, detached and re-attached with no real reason.

The deeper symbolism of form, of fold and line, is amusingly shown when men, in high positions of impressive majesty, still wear robe and gown, with the same pride that they wear trousers. The high Ecclesiastic, the eminent Judge, the College Dignitary, the King—these add to their dignity by full flowing lines, using a natural true association directly counter to the current arbitrary one.

Every kind of livery and uniform is based on symbolism, save inasmuch as it directly is modified to use. That is why American-born persons, even if they must be servants, dislike what they call "the badge of servitude," a livery.

A cook's cap, to keep the food from touching his hair—or his hair from touching the food, is a reasonable article. He doesn't wear it merely to announce that he is a cook—unless in a play. But the splash of white on the head of a "correct maid" is not a cap at all—it is only a symbol, as in the scant film of frilled muslin which passes for an apron.

Time was when dress was so heartily accepted as a form of symbolism that sumptuary laws were passed, dictating what kind of fabrics, furs and decorations should be worn by different classes.

We have nothing left of sumptuary laws except the basic requirement that people *shall* be clothed—that for reasons of modesty only.

But without law, old custom, mere habit, the long persistence of tradition, and our well-less, brainless tendency to imitate one another, keeps up the symbolic motive in our modern dress.

Chapter Two

Some Modifying Forces

ONCE recognizing that human clothing in material and structure is part of our social life; that cloth is a living tissue evolved by us for social use as much as fur or feathers are evolved for individual use; then we are prepared to recognize also the action of evolutionary forces on this tissue, in all its forms and uses.

That archaic fig-leaf story, which puts the whole burden on sex-modesty as the origin of dress, we must lay aside among other folk myths, and study the origin, development, and variation of clothes as we would study the same processes in the vegetable or animal world.

Even under the guidance of those five main lines of influence, outlined in the previous chapter, we have still many minor forces to analyze, many other influences to take into account.

Those five were but primary motives; there are many other, secondary, tertiary and so on in endless attenuation; as when for instance, a girl begs for a certain article of dress with no relation whatever to any personal feeling, but "on account of my friend's feeling."

That a human creature should have developed so subtle a social sense as this is of course proof of a high degree of socialization; but whether the reason given is absolutely honest, whether the friend's feelings are as supposed, or, further, whether these feelings, in the girl or in the friends, have any sound basis, remains to be seen.

As the modifying processes in nature are many, are complex and often contradictory in action, so we find, acting upon our clothing this same confusion and contradiction, with the inevitable results.

As for instance our general use of white for little children. This is due partly to ease in washing, but largely to symbolism. White is associated with purity, with innocence. One who had purchased a white rabbit for his little girls to play with, remarked, to a friend of mine, "Do you not think, Miss, that next to the lamb, the rabbit is the most innocent of beasts?"

Now a rabbit is no more "innocent" than a mole or a frog—and no less. But the whiteness and softness of its clothing gives, by symbolism, the idea of innocence. A Young polar bear is also white and furry; and the ermine—the last word in snowy fur—is as destructive a weasel as the great snowy owl is a destructive bird. Most polar animals are white and ferocious. Color is not innocence, nor guilt, but we have it firmly fixed in our minds that our sins, though "scarlet," shall be "white as snow"—that sin is red, or black, and virtue white.

We must admit to high place in our study of clothing the influence of economic forces; yet when this supposedly all-powerful pressure is brought to bear on clothing, it frequently fails to override any one of those more primary motives.

There was a time when the economic distinctions in dress were backed up by sumptuary laws. So sure were we that such and such garments were "suitable to the station" of such and such classes, that penalties were added for any evasions of such law.

But such psychic influences as the force of imitation and the desire to appear better than one is, as well [as] the aesthetic sense and the necessity of sex attraction, proved stronger than economic and legal pressure.

Carlyle has long since shown in his *Sartor Resartus* how frequently lacking in distinction are these "forked radishes" of human beings unclothed; and that where physical distinction does exist, it often fails to coincide with the social distinction so necessary to emphasize.[1]

Therefore, we have spent ourselves in labels and trade marks, and in the effort to keep free from imitation.

Let us take one instance of a given costume, and study the various forces which have evolved it, then combination and contradiction.

As a simple and familiar illustration, we will take the dress of an ordinary working housewife in our country, being the costume of the fifteen sixteenths of American women who "do their own work"; namely, the work of feeding and cleaning the entire family.

What is this work? In what individual activities does it consist? In what surroundings? Under what difficulties?

The work of the ordinary household consists: (a) in cooking and serving food; (b) in washing dishes, clothing and floors; (c) in dusting, sweeping and general care of the house and its furniture; (d) in sewing and mending; (e) in nursing the sick, and (f) in caring for children.

In such a melange of duties it is naturally difficult to evolve a composite costume that will be suitable to them all; especially as the economic influence, which would call for such and such an article of dress is often contradicted by other economic influences under which this wageless worker is restricted in purchase.

The fact that she is engaged in this labor proves the limitation of the family income in most cases, and beyond that immovable restriction comes the difficulty of securing a just portion of said income for her own personal expenses. If this is surmounted, comes the further difficulty that she, as a mother, finds it hard to spend on herself what is always needed for her children.

The result of this is that the predominant modifying influences governing the nature of woman's working clothes, is cheapness.

Now cheapness is merely a limitation. It has nothing to do with fitness.

The cotton print which forms the almost invariable uniform of the working housewife is, indeed, cheap, but is it, in form or substance, suitable to her occupation?

Her major business—cooking—keeps her in constant association with the stove, with fire; and not only with fire, but with food, including more or less constantly, grease.

Cotton, especially when greasy, is highly inflammable; and when such a material is presented in several layers in a loose vertical form, meets fire, the instant result is an upsweeping sheet of flame which sometimes carries death by inhalation before the victim has time to lie down, even if she thinks to do so.

The enormous number of accidents of this sort move us to transient pity, but not to thought. How seldom do we hear of men dying because their clothing is on fire. Even when it is, from the carrying of loose matches in the pocket, or the dropping of sparks from their tobacco, the smouldering blaze is easily beaten out. Close-fitting woolen or semi-woolen dress does not offer the same possibility to flame as the loose, flowing skirts and aprons of the women whose business it is to "stand over the fire" three times a day.

In the matter of fire (her constant companion) women's dress has been no farther modified than by the "tied-back apron" more common in open-grate England than here, where the iron stove is a safer cooking convenience.

Besides fire, the working housewife deals continually with water; principally dirty water. In her tri-daily dish-washing, in her weekly laundry work, in the scrubbing of floors and cleaning of windows, she is always handling water. Her cotton dress presents no obstacle at all to water. She has no oilskin coat to resist water, any more than she has a leather apron to resist fire. She simply gets wet. This experience is more frequent but less dangerous than getting burned. One direct modification to this use is shown in other lands by the "Dutch sleeve," the frank cutting off above the elbow of the arm covering of the housemaid, of the housewife who does the same work; with us the rolling up of the sleeve is the only concession.

No one who has ever observed a wash-woman with an additional layer of wet cotton apron on her wet cotton skirt, getting wetter and wetter with warm water, and then going directly out with soaked clothing and parboiled fingers to hang up the stiffening clothes in a Winter wind, can hold that women's clothes are suitably modified to their economic activities.

In the matter of dust there is less to be said, the principal objection here being in the vertical layers of skirts inviting and holding clouds of dust. Though we may not have noticed this in the woman sweeping, most of us have in the woman walking; plowing along the thick, soft dust of Summer, in a moving eddy, not a water spout, but a dust spout, raised by her feet and circulating continually among her petticoats—unable to get out. As she sweeps and dusts in the house the same result obtains, in less degree.

One excuse that may be given for this unsuitable cotton fabric in women's clothes, is that it is "easier to clean." Men's clothes would be "easier to keep clean" also if they were cotton. As a matter of fact, this quality merely adds to the labor of women—in washing and ironing the everlastingly soiled, and in remaking the continually worn out.

Another especial demand upon woman, in housework is the standing and walking, with frequent going up and down stairs.

It would be a notable scientific experiment to equip a number of men servants with the costume of women, and let them realize the additional encumbrance of these long sweeping skirts as they go about their duties.

In going up stairs the skirt has to be held up. In coming down stairs it trails along, accumulating dust. When the woman, as is so frequently the case, has the care of babies added to her household duties, this stepping about—ascending and descending—is made far more difficult by the extra burden of a child to be carried.

If the influence of economic modification were truly registered in women's clothing, whatever they might wear in the street, or for occasions of rest and pleasure (if any), they would surely wear some form of trousers in the house. The women of the harem—with nothing to do—do wear them.

Study the same economic influence on the costume of men.

No matter how rich in fabric, how voluminous and long, were the robes of the mighty, the workmen tucked up their tunics, or shortened their jerkins, and met their task in suitable apparel. The one great reason for the slow extinction of gorgeousness in men's clothing, is this modification to economic demands. Little by little the clothing of men has shrunk and dwindled to its present close casing of the limbs and body; has faded and darkened in color to meet the needs of our "coal era;" has become stiffly thick, that it might wear longer; forms now a vast standardized, dingy compromise, the visible result of economic pressure.

This is the real economic influence. It would be cheaper for a man to wear calico trousers, but not so economical; much less so.

The man's costume has its vestigal rudiments of former glories—its sword-buttons, its hint of cuffs, its furtive bits of braid or other dim adornment—but for the most part it is a rigorous and successful attempt to meet the economic activities of his life.

Not so with woman's—more primitive motives rule supreme with her. The deep root idea of sex-distinction in dress is more potent than the most glaring economic necessity.

In our own times we are beginning to see this give way—in spots.

Twenty-five years ago I dressed my little girl in knickerbockers to match her dress—no petticoat at all. A decent, pretty, useful costume.

This was greeted, then, by the contemptuous and bitter disapproval of the mothers whose little girls were, as some writer has happily put it, "like white carnations" in their many frilled skirts. Now the little girls of the wealthiest and most fashionable wear "rompers" till they are half grown up.

That baseless, brainless, useless, deadly idiocy, the long riding skirt and side saddle for women, is well on the road to extinction. To acknowledge the fact that women have two legs is no longer considered an indecency, and as they are set wider on the pelvis it is recognized that they are even better adapted for riding cross-saddle than are the narrower hipped other sex.

Now Central Park and Riverside Drive show happy girls in divided skirt, or the still better knickerbockers and long coat, riding in ease and safety, to the vast relief of the long-suffering horse.

In bathing suits we see, conspicuously, this struggle between the modifying influence of condition and action; and the reluctantly loosening grip of the older forces.

One would think that the activity of swimming, identical in every particular for man and woman, would call for a similar costume. But no—the woman must never forget that she is a female, nor that she must announce that fact.

Since we are not marine animals one would think it might be forgotten while in the water, but this is far from the case. Not only must that hoary Emblem of Sex (the skirt) be in evidence, but the woman must wear shoes and stockings as if going for a walk instead of a swim.

Bathing suits for women are made—sold, worn—in which the governing motives are Sex-Attraction and Display of Purchasing Power; and the essential needs of the occupation are quite overlooked. Ruffled and flounced, trimmed to profusion, made of costly materials—there could be no more glaring proof than this "bathing costume" of the exclusion of the dress of women from normal influences, and its almost complete exploitation for sex display.

On the other hand the man's bathing suit, woolen, for protection, dark and thick enough for modesty, and otherwise reduced to the close fitting minimum called for by the occupation, is a perfect instance of legitimate adaption. When more retired he doffs the vest and bathes in short trunks only. When with men only he bathes in the one perfect covering—his own skin. But his bathing suit does not restrict him.

In the dress of women it is interesting to mark the gradual increase of normal evolution, in spite of the continuous pressure of previous forces. This is well shown in that creation of modern times—the "tailored suit." This, with the blouse or "shirtwaist," is a frank concession to business uses. Before it we only had, for women, dresses for low-grade labor, or for ease and display. The "business suit" is a concession to the business woman. The school teachers gave perhaps the original demand for this kind of dress. Here they were in increasing thousands, in a uniform profession, having to go out of the house every day in all weathers. Later came the shop girls and office girls everywhere, with the same compulsion—to leave home daily, and to work under comparatively similar conditions.

Here the pressure of industrial evolution was strongly felt, and promptly met. The plain dark skirt and coat, the loose and comfortable waist, appeared and stayed. There is not yet such complete standardization as among men; but there is enough of it to prove widely useful.

Standardization is, in fact, one of the highest results of social evolution in dress. It is a distinction we frequently condemn as "monotonous" and "ugly"; as "destructive of individuality" and very seldom rate at its true value.

No one calls swans, greyhounds or swallows monotonous, because they dress alike; nor horses ugly, because they are not pink, blue and scarlet. To come closer, we do not condemn the toga because so many Romans wore it, or doublet and hose because they were universal in their day.

In decorative beauty our modern male costume leaves much to be desired; in mechanical adaptation it is not perfect; in color it is wearily dull, but it has one high quality which separates it by a wide gulf from that of women—its standardization.

From under-vest to overcoat any man can buy an outfit at any clothing store—within certain limits.

The result of this is that when you see a group of men together they stand out from one another by personal distinction mainly. You see the man. You look at his face, at the shape of his head, the character of his hands. If he is handsome, it is he whom you admire; not masses of hair and cloth, feathers, ribbons, jewels and veils.

If he is homely, he is not ashamed of it. He is a man, and not estimated by his beauty. He does not try to look handsomer than he is. He does not try to look younger than he is—unless in some few extreme cases of "ladykillers," or under direct economic pressure. I was told in England, that the heaviest sale of hair-dye was to workingmen.

The wide unnatural gulf between men and women, not of sex-distinction but an arbitrary distinction of status, is nowhere better shown than in dress.

Where the influences of external condition act freely upon man, they filter but slowly into the sheltered backwaters to which most women are restricted. The visible differences in date are broad enough, man's clothing responding most swiftly to necessary and progressive change; but the overwhelming preponderance of the sex motif in woman's dress is still more conspicuous.

The time-difference above alluded to does not refer to the fretful rush of "fashion," that will be discussed later; but to the fact that women's clothes remain in the farthingale period, long after men's have changed into modern times; that women preserve the muslin delicacy of "the Empire," while men are a hundred swift years onward in the plain serviceable fabrics of today. In so far as women are kept shut in, inhabiting a lesser older world, they are cut off from the health pressure of new forces, and remain, for all their capricious "styles," indubitably archaic.

The other quality, that of a glaring stress upon sex, is the major modifying force in the dress of women. We should dwell with care upon this point, in beginning, as it is so inescapable throughout our study.

First let it be clearly understood that this charge of over-dominant sex attraction in women's dress does not by any means involve a consciousness of this purpose on the part of the woman. She may and often does choose and wear her garments with no other ground of decision than that she thinks the thing "becoming" or knows it to be "stylish."

But quite unappreciated by her the designer has put into his work a more or less veiled sex appeal. Sometimes this is so conspicuous that one hardly knows whether to regard it as more obscene or ridiculous. A good type of this I once saw on an actress. The dress itself was a good one, gray in color, long and trailing, covered with a closely arranged soft glitter and fitting perfectly; but upon this pleasing ground work appeared the main outcry of the costume. Upon the front appeared three towering stalks of long stemmed flowers; black tulips or some such large and solid shape. The black stems rose from the hem and ran straight up till they stopped short with two flamboyant blossoms covering the breasts—and one just at the pelvic bone.

She might as well have had three exclamation points, three pointing hands, three placards proclaiming in plain print what the beholders were expected to think about. That of course is an extreme instance; a glaring instance, such as almost any woman would repudiate. What she does not repudiate but admires and delights to wear, is a kind of dress which emphasizes in a thousand subtle ways the fact that she is female.

Charles Reade, in his amusing short story, "Propria quae Maribus," showed that skirts were worn by women not because they were comfortable, beautiful, useful or becoming; but because the pregnant woman needed such a covering to conceal or at least to mitigate her appearance.[2]

Perhaps one does not, at first, see the logical connection, even if one admits the premise. If only the pregnant woman needs to be thus draped, why must vigorous girlhood and frail age be similarly hampered?

The answer to that is that the unfortunate or reprehensible to-be-mother must not, by adopting a special costume, suited to her needs thus call attention to her condition!

In this connection it is well to refer to the comfortable, decorous and healthful costume of the Chinese woman, the wide full trousers and long coat; and to the statement of a woman doctor long resident in China, that because of this manner of dressing she never could tell by superficial observation whether a woman was pregnant or not. Can we say as much for the skirt?

Women have first that broad demarcation—they must wear skirts; and then, ensuant, a subtle and limitless differentiation between male and female apparel, which tends to make her clothing so much thinner, softer, lighter and richer in color and decoration, that one would think men and women belonged to different species. Such distinction is sometimes seen in the birds, beasts and insects, but it is always the "sterner sex" which is labelled "male" as far as the eye can see. The female remains inconspicuous.

What modifying force is it which has so contradicted the laws of nature, so "unsexed" the human female, so forced upon her this unnatural, unfeminine decorative frenzy?

It is the one main exhibition of economic pressure upon women's dress. Man has responded to the varying demands of his numerous trades, adapting his costume to the farm or shop, to boat or horse or office, or whatever his economic environment might be.

Woman, no matter what form of labor she was expected to follow in the home, found her main line of economic advantage in pleasing man. Through him came wealth and pleasure, as also social station, home and family.

Since the remote period when man became not only prospective mate and co-parent, but prospective food supply and general source of income, women have been forced to resort to every means open to them to secure and hold one of these indispensable maintainers.

The lot of the farmer's wife was hard, but the lot of no man's wife was harder. For the unmarried woman life held no opportunities. Hence, within their iron bound limits, women were modified most by this main economic necessity, pleasing man.

This effort must perforce express itself in such channels as were allowed; and when we pass the stage of direct labor and service, the way to a man's heart through his stomach, she found the second road to a man's heart lay through his eyes.

It is not Beauty that is demanded. It is two things—variety and the visible effort to please. As one honest man explained, the reason men admire paint on a woman is because it shows her ardent wish to attract; and the cruder her performance the more plainly it shows that alone to be her motive.

In the efforts of our modern woman toward "Reform Kleider" long grown so popular in some European countries, we may observe the struggle of the true aesthetic sense, and a keen perception of hygienic and economic needs, against this overmastering pressure of sex-economic force; the wish and necessity for pleasing men.[3]

Meanwhile we have had within the last few years a period of as foolish and as extreme female costume as the world has suffered from in many years; and we have in our present slight improvement no guarantee whatever of any permanent advance.

In the heavy gorgeousness of her decorations; in her profuse beads and jewels; in rich and sumptuous stuffs and bizarre outlines; in unnecessary furs and more than superfluous feathers, we still see the woman labelling herself with a huge "W"; crying aloud to all "I am a female and I wish to please."[4]

It is a pity she often fails.

The really modern man is already far ahead of these ancient tactics, the woman still in the rear.

Chapter Three

The Principles Involved

WE CANNOT competently judge any human product without knowledge of the principles involved in its construction.

Some achievement of cookery may be offered which is beautiful to the eye, soft to the hand, agreeable in odor, and even savory to the palate, yet none of these are sufficient grounds for judgment in an article of food. It must be to some degree nutritious, or it is absolutely without value; ease of digestion and assimilation adds to that value, and it must furthermore be devoid of injurious qualities.

Again, a bridge, crossing a great river, is submitted for approval. The artist may approve of its beauty as part of the landscape; and the traveling public find it broad and easy, but unless it is sound in principles of mechanics, able to stand the pressure of the water even in times of flood; to stand the friction, the weight, the jar, of the traffic, it is not a good bridge.

Human clothing must be judged on many grounds. Its relation to life is far from simple. It must be true to the obvious requirements of immediate use, and not be false to the laws of either our physiology or our psychology.

Clothing is not only a social necessity; not only for the most part a physical advantage, and often a mechanical assistance, but it has a high esthetic value, and the closest relation to psychologic expression.

In forming definite judgments on human clothing we should be competent to measure it from many standpoints, with full knowledge of the principles involved.

Such judgment would be able to show the uselessness, the harmfulness, the ugliness, the wrongness, of many articles of dress now widely esteemed, and to lay down certain standards of measurement by which, hereafter, we may learn wisely to accept or to condemn.

Our present universal inability to form such judgment is due to general ignorance of some or all of the basic principles of right clothing. Our most common criticism rests on nothing deeper than a personal taste, itself without basis or training; and upon the quality called "style" or "fashion," a modifying influence of such importance as to call for extended treatment later.

In the disconnected efforts of "dress reformers," mainly directed toward the clothing of women, the principal issue has been the hygienic effect of given articles of costume; then the esthetic quality; and, to a very small degree, the principle of personal expression.

But no sound and thorough change can be upheld without a clear knowledge of basic laws; of the intimate relation of our clothing to spirit as well as body; of its extreme social importance, and of the real, necessity of right clothing in every relation of life.

To undertake this study we must of course have some definite understanding of the nature and purpose of human life; we cannot criticize the rigging of a ship unless we know what a ship is for.

Briefly then, for the purpose of this discussion, we will premise that:

a. Life is Growth and Action;

b. Human Life is twofold, consisting of both the Personal and the Social;

c. Personal Life demands free Growth and full Action in Personal Relation;

d. Social Life demands the free Growth of Right Social Relation, and the fullness of social Action.

Now, to descend promptly to a visible instance of the relation between clothing, and this outline of a definition of human Life; suppose a boy wears shoes, that, like those of "Uncle Arley," are far too tight.

These will, (a) hinder his personal growth; (b) interfere with his personal relationships, as in his hobbling walk displeasing the lady of his choice; (c) retard his growth in Social Relation; (d) and lower his value in Social Action by keeping him out of the association and the employment he would otherwise have attained.

This one concrete instance of the relation of a man's shoes to a man's life, is sufficient to illustrate the principles involved.

Mechanically the shoe should be durable, able to withstand moisture, cold, and friction.

Physiologically the shoe should fit the foot, leaving it room for growth while young, and for free action always.

Beyond these obvious needs we may see the effect of the man's shoes on his associates, on his own state of mind, on his employer's attitude, on his fulfillment of duty, on his social usefulness. Then, since all human conduct is to be measured ethically, and since the shoe is so necessary a condition of conduct, we may say of this kind of shoe that it is Right (for the given individual, and in given conditions) and of that kind of shoe that it is Wrong.

Returning to the above definition of human life, it is easy to see that our judgment of a given article of clothing, even when we are measuring it by personal growth and action, and by social growth and action, must still be open to wide modification in regard to *the relative values* involved at a given place and time.

As for instance, in the case of the shoe, a man might be physically uncomfortable in a tight patent leather, yet by wearing it, gain a bride, or advance in social recognition, even in securing right employment; whereas, if he wore moccasins or carpet-slippers, his physical comfort would be utterly counter-balanced by the injury to his prospects in other lines.

No aspect of human conduct is simple enough for snap judgment. The higher we advance in social organization the more complex grow our relationships. Therefore it becomes more and more necessary that we clearly recognize and firmly adhere to right Principles.

Let us now see if it be possible to indicate some reliable guides of this sort; in order to establish clear standards of judgments on clothing.

If we approach the subject from its simple side, the personal, we may build with safety on the foundation of physical health.

For the merest rudiments of animal comfort, for the fulfillment of basic physical functions, as well as for all the higher and subtler social relationships; physical health, and efficiency are essential.

We may classify our principles in this order:

Physical—Mechanical, hygienic.
Psychical—Esthetic, ethical and social.

So we may judge, from standards of the first two, that any article of clothing which injures health and lowers efficiency is Wrong. Measuring from the last three we may similarly judge an article of clothing which offends legitimate esthetic or ethical standards, or which interferes with right social development, as Wrong.

As it is always easier to judge dispassionately some wholly foreign instance, let us take a well-known one, about which we are already quite decided, and show why it is thus generally condemned. This instance is the "Golden Lily," the crippling deforming shoes so long forced upon the women of a large section of China. With perfect cheerfulness, as the article was never used by us, we agree that this is wrong; and we are perfectly correct. It is wrong by all our above-named principles; mechanically, because it grossly limits and cripples the activity of the foot; hygienically because this limitation injuriously affects the health; esthetically because the crippled foot, the shrunken leg, the hobbling gait, violate the conditions of human beauty; ethically because of the initial cruelty and lasting restriction involved; and socially because of the grotesque magnifying and perversion of sex distinction, and the interference with the sufferer's social growth and action.

Yet this custom so long maintained in China, has been thought not wrong but right; and defended, doubtless, on all the above grounds: mechanically, because it prevented the woman from escaping—made her more submissive; hygienically, as tending to maintain the delicacy and feebleness suitable to the female; esthetically, as being distinctly beautiful (?); ethically, as inducing a proper patience and endurance; and socially, as keeping women in their true relation to society—which was, entirely out of it.

It is not hard at all for us to condemn the "Golden Lily," nor to follow the clear lines of reasoning which justify that condemnation, on the above principles; but it is hard for us to put ourselves in the mental attitude of the Chinese upholders of the custom, and to follow the reasoning by which so atrocious a misuse of the human body was defended.

Again, let us take another instance from alien lands, the veiling and muffling of women in various Eastern nations.

This custom we also agree is wrong; only less so than the previous instance because it involves less initial cruelty, and is less completely crippling. It is however condemnable under exactly the same heads; from the mechanical interference with the use of the eyes, to the social error of a magnified insistence on sex and exclusion from social relationship. As in the former case, it is defended in the opinion of those nations, as wholly suitable, even necessary, to the nature and place of women.

The whole subject of the dress of women is heavily overweighed by this insistence on sex. It shows, more visibly, more constantly, than any words, how exclusively she is considered as a female; how negligible has been her relation to society as a whole. To her, the very word, Society, has been distorted and belittled. It has grown to mean, to most women, a form of amusement. They really consider the flocking together of idle people, to eat, to drink, to dance, to play cards, as "society."

To satisfy the demand of a human being for human relationship, yet at the same time to exclude the woman completely from true normal association, there has been evolved this false one, this simulacrum, this imitation "world," in which women whose husbands can afford it, find occupation and entertainment.

Other women, whose husbands are unable to afford it, look longingly upward at this game of their "superiors," and in the intermediate grades we see real intelligence and ingenuity, with a high order of persevering effort, spent in endeavoring "to get into society."

As clothing is essentially a social product, a social necessity, and as this kind of "society" is all that most women know, we find, of course, that their clothing is mainly modified to the arbitrary demands of this play-world.

In the psychology of dress we must make initial allowance for that common phenomenon of the human mind, the power of arbitrarily attaching emotional values to given acts or objects. This power is practically unlimited. Our "feelings," or mental sensations, either in passive or active form, consist of the reception or expression of energy.

Suppose a certain picture, say a "September Morn," is exhibited to a group of animals.[1] They "see" it as a patch of color, but no emotion is aroused. Now exhibit the picture to a group of men, women and children. The children see it, and understand what it is—"a lady in the water," they would call it, "with no bathing dress." The men and women seeing it would "feel" more than the children; some impressed by the tender warmth and beauty of the soft morning light, by the young grace of the bather; some, according to their previous education, by sentiments of gross pleasure, or of stern disapproval.

Many savages regard an ordinary photograph of themselves with fear and horror, believing that the spirit goes out of them to the possessor of the picture.

Religious people, in various races, regard certain pictures as sacred, and experience the deepest emotion in looking at them. This emotion of reverence is one of the most arbitrarily established and widely experienced by humanity. We consider certain objects as sacred, and experience, in regarding them, intense emotion. The child does not; but the child is taught that he must, and soon he does. We may attach this emotion to a printed book, a carved image, a stone building, a string of beads.

So with other feelings, of glory, of horror, of disgust, of fear. They are all capable of arbitrary attachment to, and withdrawal from, a given object.

In dress, as the most immediately attainable form of expression, the most universally visible, the most open to modification, we have always found a free field for emotional expression. Some of this is direct, sincere, and based on continuously acting laws. In primitive races we find it the most candid, as in the adoption of "sack-cloth and ashes" to show grief, which is only a step above the gashing of one's body for the same purpose.

As was indicated in the summary of motives in the first chapter, Symbolism is one of the strongest of the primary motives in dress, and that Symbolism ranges all the way from the crude poster effects of savagery to the most delicate distinctions between "real" and "imitation," "hand" or machine work, in our modern attire.

In this study of the principles involved in dress, we must establish some clear method for measuring the relative values of a given article or system of clothing.

In order to do this fairly, the fact of our present loose and inconsequent attachment of values must be borne in mind. Because a given people at a given time, holds a certain kind of dress as "noble," as "beautiful," as "dignified," "refined," or "proper," does not in the least make it so—see the "Golden Lilies."

We must be prepared to study our own clothing without any regard whatever to existing or pre-existing sentiment. Somewhere are to be found facts and laws underlying this great social manifestation; the facts of laws of sociology, within which we must study the action of all these principles.

The dress of women, while in large measure to be studied under the same laws as those modifying the dress of men, has two marked and interdependent distinctions; that open to any observer—the magnification of sex, and that so far less observed but even more important—the limitation of social development.

As our social relationship is the latest and highest field of human development, its demands must outweigh all others, unless they absolutely imperil individual health and development. No costume, however desirable socially, could last if it checked the growth and action of the individual beyond a certain point; but it has so far been possible, in costume as in many other fields of human expression, to maintain something quite compatible with individual advantage, yet not impeding social advantage.

The major objection to the dress of women, speaking here of that of the majority of clothed races, is that it does impede the social development of the wearer. This is its heaviest injury, even beyond the ill effects to health, the interference with comfort and freedom, the continual insistence on sex-distinction.

In facing this question we should again take note of certain peculiarities of our compound life, our individual-social existence.[2]

So long as human beings live long enough to reproduce the species the race is not extinct—see Australian Aborigines. The human race may live, individually, in great comfort, health and happiness, with a very low degree of social organization—see South Sea Islanders.[3]

A high degree of social development may be attained compatible with gross injury to large classes of individuals—see history in general, to date.

A high degree of social development may be attained, compatible with gross injury to women—see Ancient Greece, China, the Orient generally.

The highest degree of social development can never be attained without the full advantages being shared by all the competent individuals—and also, indispensably, without the full duties of that high relationship being participated in by all.

Now we are studying here the influence of one form of social expression, Dress, on one-half of the social constituents—women. As perhaps the least important among our selected principles, at least among civilized women today, let us study the mechanical conditions of their dress.

From the point of view of a mechanician, the human body is an engine of great subtlety and power, capable of wide and varied uses.

Primarily, it can stand up; it can walk, run, leap, swim, climb; it can lift, carry, pull, push, and strike; and beyond these crude primal powers lie all the exquisite subtleties of physical skill involved in our myriad crafts and arts.

Those mechanical possibilities are those of the human body, and are not by any means confined to the male body.

The mechanical distinctions of the female body enable her to bear and bring forth children; but do not thereby disable her, save in the most temporary sense, from exercise of the common human powers. It is quite true that a pregnant woman near her time cannot run as fast nor jump as far as in her girlhood, but it is not true that this temporary limitation disables her for life.

Such mechanical disabilities as belong to the female sex, woman shares with many other animals, none of whom are rendered incapable of the necessary activities of their species by the special activities of their sex. The alleged "feebleness" of women, their supposed inherent inability to do certain things, is in large measure due to the mechanical disabilities of their clothing.

We are not speaking here of health. It may be that some of the crippled Chinese women live without disease; that the veiled beauties of the harem reach hale old age; the point here urged is not of illness, but of slowness, awkwardness, weakness, tottering inefficiency.

Among our own women, in what we fondly call civilized countries, the major mechanical injury in clothing is due to three articles, the corset, the skirt, and the shoe,

The corset, in its earliest form of a "stay," or breast girdle, was a mechanical aid, as is the breech-clout to the savage. It did not affect the soft trunk muscles at all, and if not tight enough to restrict breathing or check the development of the chest, was not injurious. That ancient and sensible article we still sometimes see in use among modern dancers and gymnasts.

But the corset, in the more modern form, grew to be quite another article. Its place as a "stay" was transferred to the trunk as a whole. As a woman I knew said to a to-be mother: "If you never wore corsets before you need them now *to support your back*." The italics are mine.

It was generally supposed that a woman's body lacked the mechanical advantages of a spine, and of the supporting muscles of the trunk, and had to be reinforced by a species of permanent splint; a stiffened bandage, to hold it together or hold it up.

The mechanical effect of this bandage was precisely like that of any other tight and stiff appliance. The bound muscles were weakened, atrophied, almost lost, and the flaccid shapeless mass resultant did indeed need "support" and "form," having lost its own.

Now the muscles of the body are not mere matters of ornament, to be shaped and suppressed at will. They are parts of an intricately adjusted machine, and are all essential to the perfect working of that machine. To stunt and weaken any part of the body injures its mechanical efficiency as a whole. It need not kill, it need not even bring about disease. A bird with clipped wings may thrive and grow fat, but as a flying machine it is seriously injured.

The woman's body, as a machine, was grotesquely impaired by the corset. It could not stand as easily, or as long; it could not bend as easily—all our handkerchief-retrieving gallantry comes from wearing this article, from this idea that "it is hard for a woman to stoop." It is not hard for a woman—it is hard for a corset.

As it happens, within the last few years, those whose high mission it is to decide the size and shape of a woman's body, altering it at their pleasure, have given us first the "straight front" corset, and then that amazing object now seen in our shop windows, which runs from waist to knee, almost; which binds up hip and abdomen with steel, bone and elastic; and seems to serve principally as a supporting framework for a rigorous and complicated system of gartering.

This is purely a question of mechanics, and as such, is precisely as ridiculous and injurious on a woman's body as on a man's. Legs surely are not distinctions of sex, nor are stockings. If any man will solemnly fasten himself into one of these elaborate devices, and then try to pursue his customary avocations, he will feel at once the mechanical disadvantage resultant. If any woman, hitherto unaccustomed to such restrictions, any strong free-limbed, well-muscled normal woman, puts one on for the first time, she feels the same disadvantage.

Without touching on any other principle involved, the mechanical one is enough to show this corset as idiotic as a snug rubber band around a pair of shears.

The skirt, mechanically speaking, is only a hindrance. In its attachment it is more or less in injurious, involving a stricture around the waist muscles; in its weight it has the same effect as any other handicap to the same amount; and in its friction and pressure on the legs in motion, it forms a constant impediment.

I saw lately a moving-picture of a potato race on ice, first among men, then among women. The men, free-limbed, darted back and forth, not only with flashing swiftness, but with the grace of wheeling swallows. The women, poor things, leg-hampered from infancy, scooted awkwardly about, not only with half or less than half the speed, but with a wooden clumsiness that was positively pathetic.

And women are complimented on "grace!" A greyhound is graceful—male or female—but a greyhound in petticoats would not be graceful, nor a stag, nor a swan, nor any other living thing.

Skirted women may, of course, sit about in langorous attitudes, or stand for a while well poised. So long as no action of the legs is required, or if that action is an inch-bound walk, or swaying tassel-like motion in dancing, they may do very well, but in any movement requiring the full activity of the legs, a woman in skirts is mechanically limited, precisely as a man would be. The mincing twittering gait, supposed to be "feminine," is only "skirtine"—it has nothing to do with sex.

In recent years we have had the most conspicuous and laughable instance of this mechanical injury, in what was known as the hobble-skirt, now mercifully remitted by the Powers Who Clothe Us. Grown women cheerfully submitted to be hampered by a sheathing garment more like a trouser leg than a skirt; the extreme result of which was death from accident in many cases, death from utter inability to make a long step or leap when it was necessary; and the immediate general result of which was to make a laughing stock of womanhood. There are many deeper implications to be taken up later, but the immediate one of mechanical restriction is undeniable. It is as if we were given a single bracelet for two hands—a manacle of some six-inch freedom, so that we should have been obliged to feed ourselves with both hands at once. As complete, as contemptible was this manacle.

The other instance of our selected three is still painfully in evidence—the shoe.

I say "painfully" with intention, for the thing hurts. It hurts when one first puts it on and essays to "break it in"—as if one's shoes were wild horses! It may become passably comfortable in time, if one does not ask too much of it, but if one takes a really long walk, or if one has to "stand on one's feet," as it is so touchingly phrased, then the shoes of women are found not only mechanically defective, but sometimes instruments of torture.

Here, more simply than in either former instances, we have a perfectly defined mechanical problem.

The foot, as an engine of locomotion, is precisely alike in male and female. It may be larger or smaller, more delicate or clumsier, weaker or stronger, but as a piece of machinery it is identical.

A human foot has certain definite purposes. It is built to support the weight of the body in an upright position; to carry that body about in the process of walking, and further to aid in its more rapid locomotion. That is what a foot is *for*; to stand on, to walk, run, jump with. Anything put on the foot which interferes with these uses is mechanically wrong.

The shoes of women share certain errors in construction with those of men, but they have two gross errors all their own. One is extreme constriction of the toes, the other that indefensible outrage on human activity—the high in-sloping heel.

There is some mechanical justification for a heel—within limits. Since the stiff leather sole prevents the supple curve of the foot, the action of the real heel; the raised piece of the sole, to check a slip for instance, giving something to "dig in" with, as in descending a steep slope, is a mechanical advantage. But the moment the heel is so high as to throw the arch of the foot out of use, so small as to weaken the supporting base of the whole body, or so misplaced as to throw the weight of the body not over the heel at all, but over the instep, then we have grave mechanical injury.

All these offenses are committed in the heels of women's shoes today. The explanation is to be found under other influences, but the plain facts of this mechanical sin are indisputable.

Western horsemen wear high heels for better stirrup hold, and are frankly incapacitated for much walking.

Women's high heels have no such excuse.

They succeed in changing a dignified, strong, erect, steady, swift, capable, enduring instrument—the human body—into a pitiful, weak, bending, unstable, slow, inefficient, easily exhausted thing, a travesty on the high efficiency for which we are built.

Cruel and ignorant children have been known to force a cat's feet into walnut shells for the "fun" of seeing it totter and thump about until able to free itself. Women contentedly crush their own feet into these mechanical monstrosities and totter and thump about therein—for life.

Chapter Four

Physical Health and Beauty

IN THE efforts made in the last half century or so to "reform" the clothes of women; an effort made, as we have before stated, mainly with a view to health improvement, and secondarily for greater beauty; some natural confusion has resulted from our lack of clear understanding as to the full meaning of either.

Health, to most people, consists in the absence of disease, just as virtue is held to consist in the same negative quality—absence of sin.

The virtue of high well-doing, which often co-exists with many minor errors, we do not so popularly demand, nor the health which means the highest functioning of all our parts and processes, full-powered. As to beauty, that universal blessing, the desire of every heart, no subject of common discussion is so little understood. Yet in so concrete an instance as the human body and its clothing, we ought not to be so uncertain.

The measure of good health in a milch cow is not merely in a sleek hide and a lustrous eye, but in the amount and quality of her milk. In a horse we estimate his health not by being able to stand up in his stall and eat heartily without indigestion, but by ability to go fast and pull strongly.

A woman may be "well" in the sense of not being sick, yet remain throughout life at a grade of health far lower than was easily possible, or without ever developing to her natural power limit. Because of this we fail to appreciate the effect of articles and methods of dress which do not indeed kill, but which do check development and lower vitality.

To appreciate this we must observe the dress of women from early childhood, from where this external form of sex-distinction is prematurely forced upon little girls.

The play of young animals repeats, in free pleasurable discharge of energy, modes of action proper to their race, as cubs and kittens play at hunting and fighting, while lambs and kids merely run and jump about. In a creature of such numerous activities as man, we find the young given to an extremely varied range of play impulse, and among any set of free and active boys their play tends to develop all their muscles and to strengthen quick nervous coordination. To these processes their dress conforms.

But the dress of little girls is built on other lines. Exception being made for the present popularity of "rompers" and "knickers" among the more intelligent few, there remains a marked distinction from the time the boy is put in his first "knee-pants."

This distinction is three-fold; in material, in shape, and in *management*—in the accompanying attitudes and manners required.

In material the boy's clothing will stand more wear, and will not as easily "show dirt." The girl is still in starched white muslin, or in soft light wool or silk, while the boy is wearing heavier, darker, stronger goods. The girl's clothes are thus more liable to wear and tear, and also to appear mussed and soiled, so making work for the mother. We must not forget that fifteen out of sixteen of our mothers "do their own work," and most of those who keep servants only keep one, and have to consider her limitations of strength and temper. In either case the tendency is to check the girl's play activities in the interests of saving labor.

The shape of her garments exerts a similar influence. Because of our profound conviction that skirts are inseparable from femininity, we insist on clothing our girl children in skirts, although their constant tendency to be active has induced us to shorten them until sometimes they are absolutely broader than they are long—a mere waist-ruffle. Because of this shape come the limits in management.

Beneath these skirts the child's body is covered only with scant thin white undergarments, wholly visible unless those so-essential skirts are kept carefully vertical. Add to this our antique convictions of the extreme immodesty of the human body, and you have a steady pressure exerted on the little girl, calling upon her to "sit still," to "pull your skirt down," and generally to refrain from any action which might invert those brief hangings and expose her unexhibitable legs.

Admitting fully how much we have improved in the last few decades, it is still true that for the vast majority of our children this improvement has not been vouchsafed, almost all little girls are still handicapped from infancy by a more constant demand upon them to keep still, to behave decorously, and not to soil or tear those so easily soilable and tearable skirts. This check in the free general activities of childhood lasts through life. The vigorous girl may be a good walker; she may dance long and well, thus proving the possession of good muscles and of endurance, but she lacks that full coordination of all muscles which the untrammelled boy develops. She grows stiff sooner, ages earlier, falls more readily, is more liable to strain and sprain because of being less able to promptly recover herself in falling.

Because of her clothing and the attitudes and habits which go with it, the woman is comparatively crippled in action. Look at her getting on or off a street car, climbing up on anything, or jumping down. She may achieve it, in a determined scramble; she has the anatomical capacity, but is awkward and inefficient for lack of full exercise. We have always assumed that this was due to the physical limitations of women. It is not. It is solely due to the limitations of their clothes and of the conduct supposed to belong to them.

It is not in the nature of girl children to sit quiet and keep their clothes clean. They would keep on romping and playing as boys do; they do so keep on in the cases where they are allowed; but very early comes the parental mandate on one side and the boy's scornful repudiation on the other; after which he continues enjoying the exercises which give full free muscular development, while she begins to "sit still."

Without reference to any specific injury from a given article of woman's dress, it may be clearly shown that her clothing as a whole limits action, and so limits both health and beauty. We, as a race, live at a very low rate of activity, and of that physical beauty proper to our species. This is by no means exclusively due to our clothing, but, as distinguished from that of men, the dress of women does materially interfere with their full human development.

The single fact of the continuous soft pressure of the skirt—check, check, checking every step through life, a pressure slight in a full skirt, absolutely hindering in a "hobble skirt," is enough to alter the shape and limit the growth of the leg muscles.

A woman who in the privacy of her own home puts on a light gymnastic suit, in which to do her housework, realizes at once the previous limitation of the skirt. So does she when in mountain climbing, she goes part way, skirted, and then removes that article and goes on in knickerbockers. Even one skirt is some hindrance.

Whenever we have been forced to admit the injurious limitations of women's clothes we have met the charge by alleging it to be a necessity, or as something inherent in the nature of women, and also by our perverted ideas of beauty and decorum.

If we are not clear as to standards of human health, still less are we clear as to standards of beauty. The question of beauty, in this matter of women's clothing, is broadly divided between the beauty of the human body, with the essential distinctions of femininity, and the beauty of textile fabrics, with their mechanical and decorative distinctions.

As the simplest, most easy to establish, part of this complex subject, we will consider bodily beauty first, both as human, and as feminine. And here the aesthetist, the Hellenist, the Hedonist, may be heard in deep, well-founded complaint. Of all beauty that most surely appealing to the human perception is naturally our own. Yet we, in the course of social development, have not only lost sight of that universal joy, by covering ourselves like caddice worms with casings of other substances, but have also lost the true perception of what our human beauty is. Still further, by covering, by neglect, by our false standards, we have deeply injured our own normal development, our natural beauty, so that an ordinary human body, stripped of its coverings, is too often but a sorry thing, lean or lumpy, ill-formed, ill-connected, a pathetic object.

Physicians, who see the human body at its worst, do not attach to it the aesthetic pleasure which artists, searching always for the best, still feel.

To most of us, so powerful are the associative processes of the brain, a naked human body suggests only impropriety.

It remains true that the love of beauty is common to all of us, and that—other things being equal—the most beautiful object, to a human being, is a human being. If (that large and comforting word *If!*) we would in the first place study, understand, and fully develop human beauty; and secondly let it be seen; we might live in a world of walking statues and pictures. But these "ifs" never accomplish much.

Meanwhile, for the purposes of this treatise, we must establish some standard of human beauty with such modification as is essential to femininity, in order to show the effect upon it of the dress of women.

To escape for the moment from the confusion and prejudice so deeply covering the subject of human beauty, let us first look at the beauty of race and the beauty of sex in another species—a familiar species, the horse. Suppose we have before us, as not difficult to obtain, three pictures, representing, in identical attitudes, three race horses; valuable, successful, record-breaking race-horses; a mare, a stallion, and a gelding. As horses they are splendid specimens, all beautiful. The mare may differ slightly in appearance from the gelding; the stallion differs more markedly, but still not so much as in the least to obscure their common "points." The beauty of the horse is in certain lines, certain proportions, certain powers and methods of action, which are equine. Mare, stallion and gelding, if they are good horses, are all beautiful as horses, and so we measure them. Do we consider the stallion more beautiful than the mare because his neck is thicker and more arched, through his fighting propensities? Do we consider the mare as more beautiful than the stallion because she is relatively lighter in build? Do we consider the gelding less beautiful than either because he is merely a horse, lacking the proud mien of the male or the slimmer grace of the female?

Of course when we, the human species, judge horses, the equine species, we judge them only as a species, and the beauty we see in them is the beauty of race. If they could so judge us, and thought us beautiful—which is not likely—they would judge similarly, by race-distinction, not by sex-distinction.

But if the horses were judging one another, the mare might admire some prodigiously strong fierce thick-necked stallion, or the stallion admire some especially sleek, plump little mare, without either of them caring for the real equine standard. As for the gelding, neither would admire him, though he might be the best horse of the three. And if the stallion did all the judging, preferring and selecting mares that were small and plump and feeble, it is plain that he would at once ignore and degrade the beauty of his splendid race.

That is what has happened to humanity. When a man says, "Beauty," he thinks "woman." It is not beauty, human beauty, which he has in mind, but sex-attraction, and that is quite another matter. He had admired in the female qualities opposite to his own, and has cultivated them to such an extent as to quite forget the basic human qualities.

In a book entitled *Mrs. Walker on Female Beauty*, published in

New York in 1840, there are 400 pages of advice and suggestion devoted to "Regimen, Cleanliness and Dress," but no picture, no reproduction of a statue, no recognizing description, of any standards of beauty for the human form.[1]

Another work, *The Arts of Beauty*, by Madame Lola Montez, Countess of Landsfield, also published in New York, in 1858, gives what is called a "classical synopsis of female beauty," attributed to Felibien.[2] This is most dogmatic and particular, declaring, for instance:

> "The hair should be [*sic*] either black, bright brown, or auburn; not thin, but full and waving, and if it falls in moderate curls the better—the black is particularly useful in setting off the whiteness of the neck and skin.[3]
>
> "The eyes black, chestnut, or blue [. . .].
>
> "The eyebrows well divided, full, semi-circular, and broader in the middle than at the ends, of a neat turn but not formal."

These statements are those of personal opinion, and that well-restricted. The Countess is quite clear in her opinion of beauty at the end. She says:

> The world has yet allowed no higher 'mission' to woman than to be beautiful. Taken in the best meaning of that word, it may be fairly questioned if there is any higher mission for woman on earth.

There follows her discussion of the various arts employed by "my sex in the pursuit of this paramount object of a woman's life."

All such discussion as this treats solely of *feminine* beauty, and that not in its essentials but merely as measured by the admiration of the other sex. This standard of measurement is precisely what has so tended to exalt sex-attractiveness, and to ignore, if not distinctly injure, real human beauty.

The slightest study of the diverse customs of various races shows how arbitrarily and often how hideous, are the modifications of women's appearance demanded by the opposite sex; one simple and all-conclusive instance of which is in the artificial cultivation of mere fat; not only as among certain African tribes, where those honored by selection to become wives of the chief are confined in dark huts and fed on meal and molasses, but in far more advanced Oriental races, where the candidates for masculine favor are only less frankly imprisoned, and quite as frankly fed on fattening materials.

A slight preponderance of adipose tissue appears to be one of the natural distinctions of the female of our species, useful doubtless as part of the reserve fund for motherhood; and this initial "tendency to differ" has been seized upon by the dominant male and arbitrarily increased.

Again such practices as the removal of eyebrows, the blackening of teeth among the Japanese women; the shaving of the head and adoption of a wig among Hebrew women, although only required of wives, and probably not intended so much as an improvement to beauty as a mark of ownership, are still proof of the too effective masculine influence.

A dispassionate study of highly civilized romance, and especially of amorous verse, shows the general opinion of more modern mankind. It varies, from age to age, sometimes from generation to generation—or faster; but is always there, the powerful modifying influence of masculine preference upon feminine appearance.

At no time does there appear, either among men or among the women themselves, a clear predominant recognition of the human standard, and a measuring of women by that standard, except in Ancient Greece. The survival of Greek standards of beauty, as recognized by scholars and artists, together with their absolute and scornful ignoring of people in general, is a very pretty proof of the peculiar obliquity of our mental processes. It is, in aesthetics, precisely analogous to an ethical recognition of truth, chastity, and courage as the highest virtues by a people living contentedly as lying dissolute cowards.

If the great statue from Melos *is* beautiful, why do we not seek to approximate her proportions?[4] If she is not, why do we maintain its high position? How can we, with any faintest claim to be reasonable creatures, admire this statue, and at the same time admire the women we see about us?

The answer is not so difficult after all. The statue gives us human beauty of the highest type—that we know. It is human first, and feminine second. But what we admire in verse and prose and everyday life is merely the feminine, in such variety and to such degree as an ultra-masculine and personal taste may dictate. Always the tendency of this form of sex-selection is to magnify essential differences. If the female hand and foot are slightly smaller in proportion, more delicate in build, let this smallness and delicacy be accentuated, exaggerated—caricatured, even—to please the other sex.

As an error of beauty, already given as an error in mechanics, let us study the effect of this masculine taste on the feet of women.

The hand is preferred small, white, with slender tapering fingers; but the hand has never been as absolutely deformed as the foot because of its more obvious and varied uses. Even in China, where the foot of woman was utterly sacrificed, the hand survived, the human advantage of use was greater than the sex advantage of disuse.

But in the foot this power of sex-selection triumphed to the extent of absolute deformity. As a mechanical error it is undeniable; as a physical injury it is undeniable; as an injury to beauty it is undeniable. As a specially designed machine for a special use, the beauty of a foot is inextricably connected with that use. No ship could be beautiful the lines and general structure of which prevented her from sailing. Whenever we study applied beauty, we must measure by the uses of the object to which the term is applied.

How flat and stupid it seems to repeat a statement so obvious, so incontrovertible. If a hand is so crippled that it cannot grasp, hold and otherwise perform its functions, it is not beautiful. In proportion as its natural powers are limited, so is its beauty. We might mould it into the shape of a heart, or a diamond; we might varnish it, fix lumps or horns or tassels on it. We might make it into an object conceivably beautiful as a mantel ornament, or for hat-trimming; but it would not be a beautiful hand unless it was a usable hand.

Surely that is plain. Yet most women, following the standards set by admiring men, consider hands as beautiful in inverse proportion to their size, strength and skill; beautiful for a bleached whiteness, a smooth softness, a tapering delicacy, all of which go to prove lack of use.

The powers of a hand being so varied and so constantly in requisition—even a lady must feed herself, and sometimes use a pen or a fan—the hand has remained partly usable; but the powers of a foot being simpler and by no means as necessary, we have restricted them to a far greater degree. The hand again remains visible, at least part of the time; while the foot we have agreed to cover completely, substituting for its own shape and color the shape and color of its shell. This shell, starting its long and tortuous course of evolution as a sole-protecting sandal or a soft moccasin, has altogether forgotten its origin, and developed a technic of its own which has but the most casual connection with the fact that there is, after all, a foot inside of it. In size it must be large enough to allow of the forced insertion of the then promptly forgotten foot. In shape it must bear the general relation of being longer than it is broad—and so fastened as to stay on; but beyond that, any divigation may be allowed.[5]

To return for a moment to the more mechanical view of the subject; we stand on two legs, and our ability to balance ourselves thereon is strengthened, first, by the length of the foot, which resists the tendency to tip forward or backward; and second, by the breadth of the foot, which resists the tendency to tip sideways. If one walks on stilts one realizes the difficulty of standing still on mere pegs. Yet the preference for small feet in women ignores the value of their just proportions; somewhat in length, preferring them short; and absolutely in width, preferring if it were possible, that they should be but an inch wide.

Naturally the foot is narrow at the heel and broad across the toes—that is the shape of a foot. But it is not the shape of a shoe. The shoe insists on being pointed in front—a thing no human foot ever was. Why do we think it beautiful to make the shell of a foot so different in shape from the poor thing inside? If we take out that crushed maltreated object we find its real beauty, as a foot, is utterly sacrificed to the adventitious acquirements of the shell. Pinched, shrunken, with deformed joints and twisted toes; purple and swollen-veined from compression, it is a thing to pity and to blush for. But the proud possessor does not pity her own injured feet, nor blush for them. She has never studied the beauty of feet; she does not know or care about it. What she does know and care about is the general standard of beauty in shoes.

There is a principle involved here, as in other articles of dress later to be considered, a principle of art if not of beauty; a principle which seems to be inherent in the action of the human mind; namely—conventionalization. We recognize the beauty of certain lines and proportions in various objects, and then, subconsciously, we add them together and get their average; we seek for a common denominator; we make, from the natural object, a conventionalized design. Lotus and acanthus, iris and honeysuckle, these and many more we have frozen and exalted into imperishable units of design. This tendency has acted steadily upon the dress of women, and even upon the modification of her living body. We have seized upon certain salient outlines and proportions; and from them projected a fixed outline, representing "woman," not pictorially, but as a conventionalized decorative design.

This accounts very largely for the divigation of the shoe; and of the shoes of women more than those of men; because, as always, the man was most influenced by the necessities of human use and the woman by the necessities of sex attraction. It was more important to the man that his feet should hold him up firmly, carrying him swiftly, accurately, and long. It was more important to the woman that her feet should command admiration and so help secure her best means of support—not physical efficiency of her own, but a competent mate. The man did not have to please the woman by the small size of his feet, but by the large size of his bank account. His feet were organs of locomotion, hers of sex attraction.

Therefore in the shoes of women the element of beauty, however falsely apprehended, entered more largely, and in treatment of the shoe as a work of art, we find its danger of conventionalization.

I have been told by a highly intelligent woman, resident of one of our Southern States, that the women there will not buy shoes above a certain "number" in size; and since their feet are unaware of this limit, shoes are *misnumbered* purposely to meet the demands of this market.

This is the conventional idea of "smallness," and that of narrowness and pointedness goes with it. But the most completely idealistic extreme of this tendency to conventionalize is shown in that all too familiar addition to the foot, the "French heel." Suppose you have before you in clear silhouette a human foot, covered, as with a stocking; just the curving outline of the thing. It is rather a pleasing object, though not symmetrical. It can, possibly, be combined in repetition or some grouping for purposes of design. But the eye of the artist can improve it. Consider the object, in profile. It has a convex curve above the instep. It has a concave curve below, under the arch. It has a rounded heel. At the toe it curves up a little. Let us increase these curves, at pleasure. In the matter of toes, that little upcurve of the tip of the great toe was developed—in shoes—to the girdle-fastened toes of medieval dandies. These were not, it is true, women; but neither were they the working classes. In the matter of instep we have intensified that outline as far as we might; also as to the arch beneath; but where the pencil of the designer has moved most freely, his fancy showed the most opulent play of expression, is in the heel. The rounded outline did not please. Let us then intensify, increase, add. Not backwards—for the foot must not look longer; not sideways—for the foot must not look wider. Downwards, then, perforce. Let us add a lump, a peg, a stilt. It is not very pretty. We make it higher or lower, move it inwards, slant it, curve it—ah! at last we have beauty! The pencil, following the incurve at the ankle, the outcurve of the heel, then goes in again, farther—farther—and out again a little, at the grudgingly allowed base of this appendage. As a mere point it would really not allow the lady to stand at all; she must have at least an inch-wide thing to balance on.

So, by a perfectly natural evolution in design, we have arrived at the shape of the shining thing which stands in the shoe-shop window and is called a shoe. A slipper, a satin slipper, delicate, curved, hugging the arch beneath, gripping the toes till they are utterly forgotten in the slim point which covers them; and below instead of the unexciting slight curve of the sole of the foot, perforce, when it stands flat on the floor, we now have this languid luxuriance of graceful line, this ornamental insert between the foot and the floor, this thing we call a "heel," though it is more like a baluster or an inverted Indian club. And this we believe to be beautiful!

Chapter Five

Beauty versus Sex Distinction

IN LONDON, a few years since, 'Arry referred descriptively to his 'Arriet as "a Hat 'n Feathers." In New York the slang of the same class refers to a woman as "a skoit," sometimes even "a rag." Women do not habitually refer to a man as "trousers," or "a stovepipe."

Better proof could hardly be asked of the main purpose of the dress of women—sex distinction. Kipling, in that scornful poem of his called *The Vampire* (strange, how men object to the logical results of prostitution, yet maintain that business on the ground that they must have it!) describes the offending female as "a rag, a bone, and a hank of hair."[1] Now the bones she surely cannot help—he would have done better to have mentioned her adipose rather than osseous tissue; but the "rag" and the "hank of hair" are fairly enough rung in as distinctive attributes.

The long hair of women is one of the essential sex distinctions we insist on at present, though there was a long historic period when men, too, gloried in their flowing locks, and short hair was for slaves. Long curls are precisely as pretty, and precisely as uncomfortable and troublesome, on little boys as on little girls, but the boy resents them as early as he can, because they make him "look like a girl." We, with our exaggerated ideas of sex, hasten to differentiate the smallest children, and to keep up the distinction we make it a penal offense for one sex to wear the clothes of the other.

Yet under economic pressure or from motives of self-defense, women have repeatedly been known to wear men's clothes and so to pass for men, successfully, for long periods of time. We endeavor to increase and intensify what natural distinction there is, from ulterior motives.

In this connection the skirt is the chief item of distinction. It is the most conspicuous, and can be distinguished at the longest distance—I have read that on our wide western plains a mile is roughly measured by this: "As far as you can tell a man from a woman," meaning, of course, as far as you can tell a skirt from trousers.

More than one influence combined to evolve our trailing robes, which, as we have seen, still hold their place for kings and priests and judges. Those long flowing lines do indeed add dignity to the figure, as modern sculpture admits when it tries to make a statue in trousers; and that sense of dignity and grace does linger in our minds in connection with the once dominant sex. But there is no reason that this idea should obtain in the dress of children, or during the free coltish years of growing girlhood. Among grown women, or men either, there is no objection to these long lines being used when the symbolic purpose governs the costume.

So with long hair; there is a modicum of true aesthetic feeling in our admiration of the sleek, close-lying lines of coiled or braided hair, or of crisp curls and loose waves, yet, so far as this is genuine beauty, it is as beautiful on a man's head as on a woman's. Long hair is not a natural distinction. The mane, in so far as it is differentiated by sex, is a male characteristic, as in the bison or the lion; even tomcats have thicker hair about the neck than the female, for the same reason—protection in sex combat. But the mane of horses, used for defense against flies, is common to both sexes. It is equally common to both sexes with us; equally beautiful, equally troublesome, and equally unsanitary.

How amusing it is to hear solemn scientific men dilate on the danger of germ-carrying whiskers, even if washed daily; yet never once mention the unwashed masses of the average woman's hair. If it is well cleaned once a week, that is the exception, for most women work, and to wash their hair is an added exertion they can seldom face cheerfully.

Long hair checks activity—lest it be disarranged. I have known women, hot, dusty, cindery, on a long railway journey, refuse the luxury of an offered swim, *en route*, otherwise perfectly convenient, because it would "wet their hair."

Our assumption that long hair is beautiful is very largely an assumption. Use your own eyes, your own fresh judgment, and look carefully at the hair of all the women in the street car, or the theatre, or anywhere that you can study it.

In more than one country the women have to bear not only the burden of long hair, but—crowning absurdity—a cap to cover it, as for instance in Holland or Brittany. If they must needs decorate their heads with coif or cap, why must there be the heat and weight of long hair underneath, and the added labor of caring for it? The cap would sit lightly on short cropped hair, the woman look the same and feel far more comfortable. But neither in this regard nor any other do women reason about their costumes and customs; they merely submit to the conditions in which they find themselves.

The predominant attitude of sex distinction governs not only the shape, size, and color of women's garments, but the nature of the fabric. It would surprise us much if we found animals in which one sex had an entirely different "coat" from the other; one covered with thick fur, for instance, and the other with thin sparse hair; one having smooth, close-fitting, watertight feathers, and the other only down. Yet in this way do we delight to pile up our mountain of distinction between the sexes, till the woman in the novel is supposed to delight in laying her cheek against his "rough tweed," and the man experiences a mild ecstacy in "the frou-frou of her silken skirts." When she, for utilitarian purposes appears in tweed, she is called "mannish," or her costume is; and if he should "frou-frou"—but that can hardly be thought of! His equivalent is in the clank of steel, when weapons are worn; but without that the only noise he can make with his clothes is the creak of a starched shirt-bosom, a sound not especially alluring. If women are to be so loaded up with frou-frou that he may be pleased and attracted, why should not he carry a rattle, or wear a bell, or make some sort of noise to please and attract women?

In the human species alone the female assumes the main burden of sex-attraction, on the simple and all-too-evident ground that in the human species alone the female depends on the male for her living. To him this attraction of the other sex is naturally desirable; indeed, by nature, a far more pressing necessity than with her; but he has one all-sufficing bait which supersedes all others—the coin of the realm.

He does not have to be beautiful, or even healthy; he does not have to excel in mind or morals; he has simply to show that he can "support a wife."

We all know the other side of it, base of much comedy, as when Mr. Gilbert's legal aspirant "fell in love with a rich attorney's elderly ugly daughter." It was very amusing. The delighted father tells him: "She may very well pass for forty-three in the dusk with the light behind her." Very funny, quite absurd, clearly a contemptible thing to do; but, when the sexes are reverse, not in the least unusual.

The man has in his gift all the necessaries of life, the comforts and luxuries, the honors, too—and she, to secure these things, must first secure him. Hence that desperate efflorescence, so foreign to the real nature of women.

There is some dispute, among those who think but a little way, as to this being the cause of such feminine decoration. It is advanced, seriously enough, that women dress as they do from a disinterested aesthetic sense, and to imitate—or to outshine, other women.

As to the claim of an aesthetic sense, there is scant evidence of it. As our last chapter showed, the true beauty of the body is utterly lost sight of, ignored, and sinned against; and in choice of fabrics, in line and color, in applied decoration, the governing force is fashion, not beauty. Some fashions are beautiful, some ugly; the women show no perception of the difference.

As to imitation, it is quite true that women are imitative in dress, but not to the ultra-submissiveness of men, whose main ambition seems to be to look exactly alike, and to whom the least eccentricity in dress is anathema. A woman may wear her hair short, if she chooses, with criticism of course, and even some avoidance; but fancy a man wearing his *à la chignon!* His mates would pick at him as a flock of birds do at a stranger. It takes more strength and more courage for a man to be "peculiar" in his dress than for a woman, speaking generally.

But when it comes to the statement that women decorate themselves out of rivalry with other women, that merely admits the true cause. Rivalry—for what? For the favor of man, of course. A very obvious instance of this is in the costumes and behavior of a number of women at one of our "summer resorts" during the almost wholly feminine week, and that upon Saturday night, when the men come. Another is in the exhortation of pious advisers to married women to keep up the pretty tricks of their courtship days—to wear a rose in the hair, and so on—as they did then. To which the obvious answer is that of the man who, when similarly exhorted to maintain the gifts and "attentions" of his courting period, replied: "Why should I run after the street car when I've caught it?" Why, indeed.

But of all final and satisfying proofs on this question, the best is to study the costume effects of the class of women who most openly and helplessly live by the favor of men—who never catch the street car, but must needs continuously run after it. They make no secret of what they dress for; their rivalry is open.

Any competent inquiry must make clear the simple facts of, first, the essentially masculine nature of sex decoration; and, second, that our women have become in this sense "unsexed," having adopted a male distinction. At the same time we must recognize, under that strange disguise, the love of beauty which belongs to our race—not to either sex alone; and see further how the domestic, economic, and other limitations of women's lives have distorted that beauty sense.

The beauty of fabrics lies in color and texture, in pattern, in softness both to eye and hand, in fold and line. Both men and women feel this. As we love the ripple of long wheat in the wind, the wave motion of water, the lift and sway of leafy boughs, the soft bloom of flowers and fruit, so do we love silk and lace and velvet, soft linen and rich brocade. But where we see women, following blindly the necessity of their position, pursue it to ultimate absurdity till they carry for a handkerchief a bit of cambric and lace that no adult human being could comfortably blow his—or her—nose in once; or till they put on for underclothes mere cobwebs of flimsy lace and ribbon—things no stretch of imagination can call garments—then we see true beauty sacrificed to sex.

Men's clothes, with all their limitations and absurdities, have one main advantage—they are standardized. Let no one imagine that this criticizing of the dress of women involves any claim of perfection for the dress of men. The stiff ugly trousers that bind the knee in sitting and are liable to split when the wearer suddenly squats; the coat, which must be taken off in order to do any active work; the hard, stiff, heavy hat, with its "sweat band," and its concomitant of baldness; or—to consider other races—the Oriental custom of shaving the head and then wearing a turban (a thing quite as absurd as the heavy hair of women with a cap to cover it all) the dress of men, in general, is by no means an ideal. But such as it is, it is standardized. It is practically uniform, and The Man is noted rather than the clothes.

Because of this standardization the burden of choice is very greatly lightened. A man, of similar class and character, does not have to give a tenth part of the time and thought to his dress that is required of a woman. Neither is he judged by his dress as is a woman. Many a great man is described by his admiring biographer as "careless, even slovenly, in his dress," and though there is room for criticism on the ground of neatness—all preferring to see clean clothes on man or woman—we do not superciliously criticize a man because he "does not know how to dress," as we do a woman.

The woman's dress, her sex-specialized, highly decorative dress, has been identified with her womanhood, and she is condemned for falling short in this supposedly "womanly" attribute; whereas in fact this extra decorative effort is essentially masculine. Our women, in their "war-paint, beads and feathers," have become so far male; and our men, in their contented serviceable obscurity, have become so far female.

If the feeling of women was for beauty, real beauty, applied to the human form in combined fabrics, we should present a very different spectacle. Again and again, in the history of costume we have seen beauty; types of dress which blessed that age or race and have remained to us in picture and statue. But they never stayed. There was no true perception, no joyful recognition of and insistence on the principles of beauty. Many races have evolved a permanent costume, especially among peasants; but with some beautiful features they also preserve grotesque, ugly, uncomfortable, or unhygienic ones, with equal pride.

No costume for women has been evolved which is more convenient, decent, comfortable, and, in its own way, beautiful, than the Chinese. Yet that very nation, on those very women, also evolved that unforgivable monstrosity, the "Golden Lily."

There will be much to say in the course of this work, on Fashion, and in this chapter belongs the treatment of the contributing influence of sex-distinction to that Undisputed Power. Its economic and psychic aspects will be discussed later.

If the arbitrary changes of Fashion were common to the race we should find them followed by men as conspicuously as by women; but when we see as marked a difference as exists between the sexes in this regard, we must look for the cause either in some essential distinction between the two, or in a variation based on special conditions affecting one of them.

It is clearly to be seen, in our time and country, as in most of the more advanced races of the world, that the "fashions" in women's clothes are (a) more numerous and varied—see the tremendous sale of "patterns" and of magazines which live largely on the sale of said patterns; (b) more rapid in change; and (c) are studied and followed by a far larger proportion of the wearers.

Men are not averse to studying their own fashions, especially when young and "in love," but in a given number of men and women not young and not in love, a much greater proportion of the latter will be found studying the "fashion page."

This our easy androcentric view has casually set down as "woman's weakness"; whereas we need to learn how this bit of man's weakness has been so completely transferred to the other sex. If we study it for the moment, in him, as among the unblushing gorgeousness of savage "bucks" and the discriminating splendor of a Beau Brummel, or a "Sir Piercie Shafton," we may begin to trace the line of evolution.

The primitive male exhibits his natural sex tendency in decoration as innocently as any peacock; and so do more sophisticated males under conditions which allow it. Blazing masculine splendor, with velvet, embroidery, jewels and lace, was found among men who did not "have to work"—knights and nobles and "gentlemen." The gradual development of our present economic era, where work and manhood are almost coterminous; and where, as with us, it is a point of masculine pride to maintain women in idleness, or at least in domestic industry without pay, shows us the original characteristics completely changed. The man now, instead of laboriously developing crest and wattle, mane and tail-feathers on himself, or their equivalent in gorgeous raiment, now exhibits them on his woman.

It is pathetically amusing to see the struggle between a man's human common sense, expressed in his opinions about women's clothes, and his masculine instinct, expressed in his actions. His critical human judgment loudly complains of the vanity of women, the extravagance of women, the women's silly submission to fashion, but his male instinct leads him straight to the most vain, extravagant and fashionable of them all.

Women are not fools, nor are they so vain as is supposed. Vanity, from prancing stag to strutting cock is inherently male. Never a female creature do you find that can be called "vain" till you come to woman, and her so-called "feminine vanity" is by no means inherent, but acquired under the pressure of economic necessity.

Let a man try to put himself in the place of a young woman, with every chance of "fun," all his good times, all his opportunities to go anywhere, to see anything, to dance, to ride, to walk even—in some cases, depending on some girl's asking him![2] Suppose the girl was the one who "had the price." He would have then to please the girl—naturally. He would have not only his natural impulse in that direction, but this new and heavy necessity. This is what has happened to women for thousands of years. There was no liberty for woman. It was a man's world, and not safe for her to go about in. She was liable to be attacked at any time, by one of her "natural protectors." Except under his escort she was housebound, a prisoner.

All this is as a mere aside from that still more vital necessity of securing a permanent livelihood by marrying, and the natural desire to please the one you love.

The way to a man's heart, we are told, is through his stomach, and we sagely add: "Every woman should know how to cook." But the shortest route to a man's heart is through his eyes. We have no record of the culinary skill of Cleopatra, or Ninon de l'Enclos, or Madame Recamier.[3] There have been millions of assiduous female cooks—but the record heart-breakers, from Aphrodite down, did it by good looks.

We are not all born beautiful; neither do we all have by nature that capricious charm which holds the vacillating fancy of the male. One of our amiable androcentric proverbs is that women are eternally changeable—"varium et mutabile." Yes? Are *other* females? In other races the male, the naturally variable factor, changes and fluctuates as he may, so offering choice to the female; she, the natural selector, thus by discrimination, improving the race. But with us we find him doing the choosing, and we find the woman, depending on his favor not only for mating, but for bread, caters to his taste by this admired capriciousness.

Let it be clearly understood that it is *not* a pleasure to all women to spend their lives in an endless and hopeless pursuit of new fashions—like a cat chasing her tail. It adds heavily to the care, the labor, the expense, of living. It is a pitiful, senseless, degrading business, and they know it. But let one of them be misled by man's loud contempt for "the folly of women"; let her show originality in design, daring in execution; let her appear in public in a sensible, comfortable, hygienic, beautiful, but *unfashionable* costume—! Do the admiring men flock to her side? Do they say: "*Here* is a woman not silly and sheep-like, not extravagant and running after constant change!"? They do not. If they are near enough to feel responsible, they murmur softly: "My dear—I hate to have you so conspicuous. A woman must never be conspicuous." If very honest, they may add: "It reflects on me. It looks as if I couldn't afford to dress my wife properly." As for the others—they simply stay away. With lip-service they praise the "common-sense" costume, but with full dance cards and crowding invitations they pursue the highest-heeled, scantest-skirted, biggest-hatted, "very latest" lady. (At this date, April, 1915, "skirts are fuller," hats very small, and we hear "the small waist is coming in again"!)

Women are foolish, beyond doubt, but they are not nearly so foolish as they look. Those "looks" of theirs, especially in the matter of ever-changing dress, are most valuable assets. Now let no woman take this as a charge of deliberate calculation. It is nothing of the sort. It is an "acquired characteristic" of the female of genus homo, quite unconscious. But it is by no means a "feminine distinction." When women have freed themselves from their false and ignominious position of economic dependence on men, then they can develop in themselves and their clothing, true beauty. They will then recognize that since the human body does not change in its proportions and activities from day to day, neither should its clothing; that if the eye of the observer craves variety, or the mood of the wearer, this may be found legitimately in color and decoration, without the silly variations which make of that noble instrument, the body, a mere dummy, for exhibition purposes.

As we read in the old ballad:[4]

> "When I was aware of a fine young man
> Come frisking along the way.
> The youngster was clothed in scarlet red,
> In scarlet fine and gay."

Then, on the day following, was seen:

> ". . . the same young man
> Come drooping along the way.
> "The scarlet he wore the day before,
> It was clean cast away,
> And at every step he fetched a sigh—
> 'Alack! and 'Ah-well-a-day!' "

Here we have the legitimate change wherein the costume expresses the mood, a need by no means limited to either sex. That we should always be free to use. In our artificial sex distinction in dress, we have robbed ourselves of the highest beauty in both. We have cut off all the haughty splendor natural to the male, which should rejoice the hearts both of the man in joyous exhibition and of the woman in her glad observance. Nothing is left him but the insignia of office—which he fondly cherishes, and the foolish sashes and aprons of his secret societies. It is a pity, a great pity, to rob mankind of its instinctive glory, and womankind of glad appreciation. The world is starved in beauty because of it.

Then further, by foisting upon woman this unnatural display—display which is governed by the easily jaded fancy of the capricious male, we have left ourselves, instead of beauty, this uneasy flutter of signals, this mad race of ceaseless changes, each crying louder than the last: "Look here! Look here!"

If women had, as some allege, an instinct of beauty, they would never allow themselves to exhibit the gross excesses, the jarring contradictions, the pathetic, thread-bare, hardly veiled appeals, of their man-designed clothing. If sex distinction were working normally, women would demand in men a rich variety, a conspicuous impressive beauty. The world would throb and brighten to the color music of Nature's born exhibitor, the male.

Then further, that same normal distinction would strike the true note of womanhood, and give us another beauty, restful and satisfying. It is woman, the eternal mother, who should express peace and power in her attire, not glitter like a peddlar's tray, to catch the eye. In her flowering girlhood she should be lovely as an unblown bud, with all the delicate shades of mood and fancy, and in that long and splendid period of exclusively human life, after she has outgrown the limitation of sex, then indeed she should make it part of that human life to express the highest beauty.

But now! Now we must bear the sight of women, young and old, degraded from their high estate—the choosing mothers of the world, and instead, in garb and bearing, become themselves the caterers, the exhibitors on approval.

That men want it is too clearly proven by their constant efforts in design. That men like it is clearly proven by their admiration of the "stylish" woman, their neglect and avoidance of the woman who dares dress otherwise. But that in the face of these facts, they should so naively speak of "feminine vanity," "feminine love of change," and the like, and joke serenely, about the "feminine love of shopping," is unworthy of "the logical sex."

Women do spend more time and take more pleasure in the consideration, examination, and purchase of clothes, than do men; but observe men in the act of buying a horse, or a boat, or a gun, or a fishing rod—they will "shop" some time in these processes, and enjoy it.

Our common ideas of sex distinction are both exaggerated and incorrect. There is by no means as much of it as we suppose. Our human qualities which we hold in common are far more numerous and important than our sex qualities, which we hold separately. Further, our generalizations on the subject are quite wide of the mark and sometimes flatly opposite to the truth, as in this idea of "feminine vanity."

And nowhere do our errors on this subject speak more loudly, show more clearly, than in dress. When we shall have reached greater wisdom, when we know the difference between sex qualities and race qualities, between the essentially male and the essentially female, between the force of a natural attraction and the force of an economic necessity, then we can manifest our higher stage of progress in a far more legitimate and also more beautiful costume. Certain essentials will be observed, as of modesty, warmth, suitability to various trades; certain distinctions proper to sex, as in the greater gorgeousness and variability of the male; but the major note will be adaptation to the human body and its activities.

Holding fast to this, our aesthetic sense will work hand in hand with truth and need, as it should; and we may so develop costumes as lovely and as serviceable as the plumage of a swan, the shimmering scales of a fish.

There will be room, too, for the subtlest play of personality, or original fancy, far more so than at present. Free bodies, honestly expressed spirits, needs well met, and all the lovely play of fresh invention, unforced but welcome, will give us a world of beauty in human dress such as we have not yet dreamed of.

Chapter Six

The Hat

IN NO one article of dress is the ultra-feminine psychology more apparent than in the hat.

For man or woman, the head covering has always been used far more for symbolism than for any of the other basic motives. As a head covering the natural one, hair, has for the most part remained to women. Men, having decided to curtail their hair, demand more of their hats in the way of covering.

It may be as a protection from sun and wind, and it may be as a lingering rudiment of that ancient psychology of sex which gave to the man his distinctive head-dress, and, owing to which, he still feels less a man when hatless. "Where's my hat?" is the frantic demand of the small boy. Be he never so much in a hurry he does not feel truly himself unless that inconspicuous, small, often ugly and shabby, but indispensable mark of masculinity, is on his head.

Boys in their continuous scuffling "play," that innocuous infantile survival of the ancient sex-combat, are particularly merry with one another's hats. To snatch off the other boy's hat; to hold it, hide it, trample it; is a favorite form of amusement. The boy thus rudely unhatted must fight for his lost distinction, and does so cheerfully.

In the attitude of children toward their clothes we may all too plainly see the proof of the long dominance of the sex motive in our attire; the girl child, trained, flattered, and punished into a premature care of and pride in her over-feminine apparel; and the boy child, needing neither praise nor blame to develop his perfectly natural masculine vanity in the garments which proclaim him Man. His are, to be sure, of a far ruder and more serviceable sort than hers; but his joy in them, his irrepressible pride, is not based on their practicality so much as on their proof of what he fondly imagines to be sex-superiority.

In the matter of hats, the scope of masculine expression is not large. A hat he must have, of severe and simple outline. In it he may express, (a) sex; and (b) wealth; also, to a very limited extent, personal taste. Those who dwell in detailed admiration on the dress of men speak mainly of the cut and line of their garments, the taste shown in those minor accessories of socks, ties, and a man's scanty but impressive jewelry.

When they refer to his hat there is nothing to gloat upon but its newness, both in style and recent purchase. The top-hat has always its clear distinction; the crisp straw in summer, the hard hat with the latest roll brim—there is little to boast of. The man, in selecting, tries to choose one suited to his particular style of feature, and sometimes succeeds. So choosing, he generally remains constant to that choice.

We must remember that a man's sex-value does not lie in his beauty so much as in his purchasing power and in the general qualities pertaining to masculinity—or supposed so to pertain.

With the woman it is widely different. While every article of her attire, from the innermost to the outermost, is modified not only by sex-distinction but by the constant fret of change in order to please and hold the varying taste of the male; the hat more than any other article shows this double pressure.

With our naive effort to preserve by force the artificial distinctions with which we have fenced off one sex from the other, we consider it quite incorrect for a woman to wear a man's hat; for her merely to try one on is supposed to give him the right to kiss her. But still, though for riding costume, yachting costume, and such limited purposes, we do find women wearing men's hats, or hats frankly mannish in style, we do not, for any purpose whatever save those of roaring farce and coarsest circus humor, find men wearing women's—to make themselves look ridiculous.

When a woman puts on her husband's silk hat or "derby," soft felt or stiff straw, she may look "mannish," but she does not become a laughing stock. When a man puts on his wife's "Easter bonnet," big hat with flowers and ribbons, or small hat with some out-squirt of stiff or waggling decoration, he looks contemptible or foolish.

There is real reason for this. The man's hat, whatever its fault, has a certain racial dignity. It is, primarily, a covering for the human head. It is designed to fit that head. It is simple and distinct in outline, restrained in ornament.

None of these things are true of the woman's hat, which, whatever its attractions, is utterly lacking in that main attribute of racial dignity. It is not, primarily, a covering for the human head. It is not in the least designed to fit that head. It is not simple and distinct in outline; and—need it be said?—it is not restrained in ornament. A woman's hat may be anything—anything in size, in shape, in substance, in decoration. Its desirability is based on three necessities; first, it must be "stylish"; second, it must be new; third, it must be "different"; not only different from the previous one, but different, as far as is compatible with style, from the hats of other women. We might add, as a remote fourth, a faint preference for a hat which is "becoming."

To discover a hat which suits the face of the wearer, which is light and easy on the head, and to wear the same sort of hat as long as one has the same sort of face, would surely be a reasonable thing to do. That is it would if the purpose of a woman's hat was to make the wearer comfortable and to express personality. Nothing is farther from its purpose. The first, last, and ever dominant necessity is to express as loudly as possible, not the "eternal feminine," but that abnormal pitiful femininity of ours, a femininity which has surrendered its solemn grandeur of womanhood, and put on, jackdaw-like, the ostentatious plumage of an alien creature.

Study the grave sweet face of some eternally beautiful woman-statue, as of our so familiar "Mother of the Gods," miscalled the Venus of Melos. Put upon that nobly feminine head some "cute," "too sweet," "charming," "latest thing," and see how utterly out of place is such monkeyish display on real womanhood.

"Yes," we admit, "but women don't look like that now. I'm sure Dolly Varden looks just too sweet for anything in that hat."[1]

A pretty child—of either sex—looks pretty in almost anything. Some fresh-cheeked, curly-headed boy may look as well as his sister with a frill of lace and roses around his face. But a grown woman, a woman fit for motherhood, is no longer a child. Her place in life is as gravely important as her husband's. Even a young girl, with wifehood and motherhood before her, has a potential dignity, a high responsibility awaiting her, beside which all this capering and fluttering of gay signals is pathetically ignominious. We have enough instances before us, in marble and canvas, in tender madonnas, brave-eyed saints, great goddesses, to show this truth. We have behind that the whole long story of unfolding life on earth, the female earnest and plain, the male skipping and strutting in gay adornment. Even the male mosquito has feathers on his head—not the female.

In ordinary life we have the well-known fact of the lasting beauty that shines in such severe simplicity as the white face-bands of the nun, or in many of the neat and unchanging caps worn by Puritans, Quakers and others. We even know, in that remote shut-off compartment of the mind wherein we keep our articles of faith, that "Beauty unadorned is adorned the most."[2]

Beauty, however, is far from our thoughts. With serene unconscious fatuous pride our women put upon their heads things not only ugly, but so degradingly ridiculous that they seem the invention of some malicious caricaturist. In ten years' time they themselves call them ugly, absurd, and laugh at their misguided predecessors for wearing them. If honest and long-memoried, they even laugh at themselves, saying: "How could we ever have worn those things!" But not one of them stops to study out the reason, or to apply this glimmer of perception to the things she is wearing now.

Any book on costume shows this painful truth—that neither man nor woman has had any vital and enduring beauty sense; and further that while man has outgrown most of his earlier folly, woman has not.

There is today no stronger argument against the claim of Humanness in women, of Human Dignity and Human Rights, than this visible and all-too-convincing evidence of sub-human foolishness.

In other articles of costume there have always been certain mechanical and physiological limitations to absurdity. In hats there are none. So that the wearer is able to carry it about, so that in size it is visible to the naked eye, or capable of being squeezed through a door—with these slight restrictions fancy has full play, and it plays.

The designer of women's hats (let it be carefully remembered that the designers and manufacturers are men) seem to sport as freely among shapes as if the thing produced were meant to be hung by a string or carried on a tray, rather than worn by a human creature. There is a drunken merriment in the way the original hat idea is kicked and cuffed about, until the twisted misproportioned battered thing bears no more relation to a human head than it does to a foot or an elbow.

The basic structure of a hat is not complex. Its ancestry may be traced to the hood, coif, cap, the warm cloth or fur covering, still shown in "the crown"; and to the flat spreading shelter from the sun, now remaining in "the brim." In simplest form we find these two in the "Flying Mercury" hat, a round head-fitting crown, a limited brim. The extreme development of brimless crown is seen in the "night-cap" shape worn by the French peasant, the "Tam O'Shanter" of the Scotchman, the "beretta" of the Spaniard, or the "fez" of the Turk. The mere brim effect is best shown in the wide straw sun-shield of the "Coolies."

Among the Welsh peasant women we find the crown a peak, the brim fairly wide; among priests, Quakers, and others, we find a low crown and a flat or rolled brim; in the "cocked hat" the brim is turned up on three sides; the "cavalier" turned his up on one side and fastened it with a jewel or a plume. Among firemen and fishermen the brim is widened at the back to protect the neck from water.

There is room for wide variation in shape and size without ever forgetting that the object in question is intended to be worn on a head. But our designers for women quite ignore this petty restriction or any other. I recall two instances seen within the last few years which illustrate this spirit of irresponsible absurdity.

In one case the crown was lifted and swollen till it resembled the loathsome puffed-out body of an octopus; and this distorted bladder-like object was set on an irregular fireman's brim—to be worn sideways.

For forthright ugliness this goes far, but here is one that passes it for idiocy:

Figure to yourself a not unpleasing blue straw hat, with a bowl-shaped crown, setting well down on the head, and a plain turn-up brim about two inches wide. Then a grinning imbecile child gets hold of it. With gay grimaces he first cuts the brim carefully off, all of it, leaving the plain bowl. Then, chattering with delight, he bends the brim into a twisted loop, and fastens it across the "front" of the inverted bowl, about halfway up. There it sticks, projecting like a double fence, serving no more purpose than some boat stranded by a tidal wave halfway up a hillside. And this pathetic object was worn smilingly by a good-looking young girl, with the trifling addition of some flat strips of blue velvet, and a few spattering flowers—all as aimless as the stranded brim.

Five years ago it was customary for women to wear hats not only so large in brim circumference as to necessitate tipping the head to get through a car door, but so large in crown circumference as to descend over the eyebrows, and down to the shoulders. These monstrosities were not "worn"; they were simply hung over the bearer as a bucket might be hung over a bedpost. And the peering extinguished ignominious creatures beneath never for one moment realized the piteous absurdity of their appearance.

Yet it is perfectly easy to show the effect by putting the shoe on the other foot—that is, the hat on the other head. Imagine before you three personable young men in irreproachable new suits of clothes, A., B., and C. Put upon their several heads three fine silk hats, identical in shape and style, but varying in size: upon A., at the left, a hat the size of a muffin ring, somehow fastened to his hair; upon B., in the middle, an ordinary sized hat, fitting his head perfectly; upon C., at the right, a huge hat, a hat which drops down over his ears, extinguishes him, leaves him to peer, with lifted chin, to see out from under it in front, and which hangs low upon his shoulders behind. Can any woman question the absurdity of such extremes—on men?

When some comic actor on the vaudeville stage wishes to look unusually absurd, he often appears in a hat far too large, a hat which, seen from the back, shows no hint of a neck, only that huge covering, heaped upon the shoulders. In precisely such guise have our women appeared for years on years, with every appearance of innocent contentment—even pride. They had no knowledge of the true proportions of the human body, the "points" which constitute high-bred, beautiful man or woman. They did not know that a small head, one eighth the height of the person, was the Greek standard of beauty; that a too large head is ugly, as of a hydrocephalic child, or of some hunched cripple whose huge misshapen skull sits neckless, low upon his shoulders. They deliberately imitated the proportions of this cripple. Seen from behind a woman of this period was first a straight tubular skirt, holding both legs in a relentless grip, as of a single trouser; then a shapeless sack, belted not at the waist, but across the widest part of the hips (a custom singularly unfortunate for stout women, but accepted by them unresistingly); and then this vast irregular mass of hat, with its load of trimming, as wide or wider than the shoulders it rested on. In winter they would add to this ruthless travesty of the human form by a thick boa, stole, or tippet, crowded somehow between shoulders and hat, so that you could see nothing of the woman within save her poor heel-stilted feet, the strained outline of those hobbled legs, and part of the face if you ducked your head to look beneath the overhang, or if she lifted her oppressed eyes to yours.

At present the Dictators of our garments have changed their minds and we are now for the most part given hats of the most diminutive size, whose scant appearance is "accented" by some bizarre projection, some attenuated crest of pointed quill, or twiddling antennae.

What accounts for this peculiar insanity in hats? Why should a woman's hat be, if possible, even more absurd than her other garments? It is because the hat has almost no mechanical restrictions.

When a woman selects a hat; when she tries one on, or even looks at one in a window, she sees in that hat, not a head-covering, not her own spirit genuinely carried out through a legitimate medium, but a temporary expression of feeling, a mood, a pose, an attitude of allurement.

The woman's hat is the most conspicuous and most quickly changed code-signal. By it she can say what her whole costume is meant to say; say it easier, oftener, more swiftly. Because of this effort at expression, quite clearly recognized by the men who design hats, they are made in a thousand evanescent shapes—to serve the purpose of a changeful fancy. Did he see her in this and think he knew her? He shall see her in that and find she is quite different. Man likes variety; he shall have it.

Meanwhile there is no article of dress more easily judged by legitimate principles of applied beauty than is a hat. Whatever else it may be for, it is to be worn on the head. The head is not a sex-characteristic—it is a human characteristic. The dignity, the intelligence, the superiority of our race is shown most of all in the head; not only in the face and its frontal crown—the forehead, but in the size, shape, and poise of the head itself.

All these human characteristics are the same in man or woman. Therefore we may lay down this clear and simple principle for a head-dress—a legitimate and beautiful one looks equally well on man or woman. A fillet, wreath of laurel, garland of roses, circlet of gold, or crown of jewels—these look equally well on man or woman. Any hat or head-dress of simple lines, evolved for legitimate purposes, looks equally well on man or woman. The Tam O'Shanter, Glengarry, fez, turban, wide-brimmed "shade hat," or close-fitting "polo cap," soft plumed "cavalier" or smart "sailor"—these are coverings for the human head—not sex-signals, though any of them may be made such by mere usage, and a false standard of taste rapidly developed and arbitrarily attached to them. But the Roman general was not made feminine by his rose-garland, nor Sappho masculine by her wreath of bay.

"But there must be sex distinction in dress!" some will protest.

Granting for the sake of argument that there must be some, the question then arises—how much? Should a hat say, "I am a head-covering," or should it say, "I am a signal of distress—come and get me."

Granting, more fully and frankly than above, that there should be sex-distinction in dress, it should be *legitimate* sex-distinction. It should show the real nature of the sex represented. Women have yet to learn the true characteristics of their sex—and of the other. Let them study any other species of animal they choose, and see the male, always the male, flaunting his superfluous plumage, strutting and crowing, stamping and bellowing, hopping and prancing about, to say nothing of his valorous combat with his rivals, all to attract the attention and win the favor of the observant female.

She does not do all this. Never a female in all the world do we see flourishing unnecessary feathers, erecting haughty crests, shaking gay wattles, capering and posturing to attract the attention and win the favor of the male—never one but the Human Female.

We have to learn that all this gay efflorescence and frisky behavior is *not* feminine—it is masculine. Our position is analogous to that of a pea-hen who has somehow secured the gorgeous tail-feathers of her mate, and is strutting about to attract him—a thing any pea-hen would be ashamed to do.

She does not have to. She is The Female, and that is enough. It is her Femininity that attracts, and no amount of borrowed masculine plumage adds to that inborn power.

If a woman wants to judge her hat fairly, just put it on a man's head. If the hat makes the man look like an idiot monkey she may be very sure it is not a nobly beautiful, or even a legitimate hat. If she says: "Oh, but it is so cute on me!" let her ask herself: "Why do I wish to look cute? I am a grown woman, a human being. Mine is the Basic Sex, the First, the Always Necessary. I am the Mother of The World, Bearer and Builder of Life, the Founder of Human Industry as well. My brother does not wish to look 'cute' in his hat—why should I?"

Women, supposedly so feminine, so arbitrarily, so compulsorily feminine, so exaggeratedly and excessively feminine, do not realize at all the true nature, power and dignity of the female sex. When they do, even in some partial degree, there will be nothing in the long period of their subservience upon which they will look back with more complete mortification than their hats.

In the matter of the "Golden Lilies" they had no choice. In the matter of the veil, the "Yashmak," they had no choice. In the matter of shoes—save by a lifelong wrestle with obdurate shoemakers and shopmen—they had no choice. But in the matter of hats they *had* choice—and they chose with enthusiasm and ardor, at great expense, too, and with pitiful teasing and persuasion, the most monstrous, silly, useless headgear the market afforded.

We may show that men designed them; we may refer back to the man's taste that admired them on feminine heads; but that does not alter the fact that millions on millions of women, contentedly, gladly, proudly, bought and wore them.

Women of today are educated. They study Art, art with the largest of *A's*, the longest of histories. They admire, or profess to admire, the still beauty of great statues and fragments of statues which have remained to us from the past. But they have not so much as tried to apply any known principle of beauty to their own garments, selecting and commending them only from a baseless notion of what is "becoming" among the arbitrary list of "styles."

While speaking of women's hats another point is worth mentioning. The size and widespread decoration of these objects, together with the custom of wearing them in houses, has long since made them a cruel nuisance where there was anything to be seen. In theatres for instance, for years and years, calm well-bred women would sit hatted through a performance, *knowing*, sometimes through protest of the sufferer, that the man behind could not see the stage on account of that huge headgear. At last this custom was forcibly ended, not by any reason or mercy on the part of the women, but through regulations enforced by the management. In churches they are very slow to adopt this wise and courteous custom of hat-doffing, on account of quotations from Hebrew personages of some two thousand years past.

"The glory of a woman is her hair," said one of these ancients. "Let your women be covered in the churches," said another.

The glory of a woman is not her hair today; it is her hat. If Saint Paul had seen our Easter display he would have said: "Let your women's hats be covered in the churches." But we do not reason about these things.

In the theatre we can hear something, even if we cannot see. In the church or concert-hall, we can hear, even if we cannot see. But what shall we say of a woman, a kind, sympathetic, well-bred woman, who will go to a *baseball game* and wear a big hat? They do it. I have seen three vacant seats behind a big-hatted woman at a ball game; good seats too, in a crowded stand. Now what, if anything, was going on in that woman's head? Did she not *know* that the one essential in a ball game is To See? Did she not *know* that there were men behind her, eager men who had paid for their seats? Did she not *know* that she had no more right to put a yard of hat-brim in front of their eyes than a yard of newspaper or an open umbrella?

Which reminds me that I have seen "the gentler-sex" sit under open parasols in the crowded best seats at an exhibition of outdoor sports!

One further proof—if more were needed—that women's hats have entirely lost their original purpose of head-covering from sun or cold, appears in their present custom of wearing hats in the house for decorative purposes merely, not only in the church, under direction of the Ancients; not only in public places where no convenience is provided for laying off these cumbrous adornments; not only in brief "calls," and the more or less transient "tea" or "reception"; but in the prolonged intimacy of a luncheon, in private houses, where they go upstairs and "lay off their things"—their other outer garments, and then solemnly maintain their supposedly decorative hats. About the table they sit, long plumes and lofty twiddlers waggling, getting in the way of the waiters, often making the wearer's head ache—and all for no shadow of reason.

This is a "ladies luncheon," mind you. They do not have to charm each other. As far as mere flourish of trumpets goes they exhibited those hats when they came in, and will again when they go out. There was a place to put them, and plenty of time to take them off and put them on again. As for that shamefully mortifying excuse that their hair is not properly arranged—surely a lady who has time to dress for a lunch-party has time to comb her hair.

This one instance of the brainlessness which distinguishes the dress of women, supereminently exhibited in the matter of hats, ought to be convincing enough, if we had no others. That those who exhibit this lack of applied intelligence may be otherwise women of good mentality, perhaps of wide education, proves no more than that oft-established fact of human psychology—that the human brain has an enormous area, and that full use in some departments is compatible with total neglect in others. Some of the wisest and greatest of men have not had sufficient intellectual ability to leave off the childish excesses of gluttony, or the more dangerous drug habits. Some of the best and most brilliant of women have not sufficient intellectual ability to wear hats worthy of womanhood, or to take off their unworthy hats in the house.

Even this short commentary upon women's hats is incomplete without reference to one of their most insolent, cruel and offensive features: the use of pins and decorations which tickle, irritate, and sometimes painfully injure other people.

If some gaping imbecile or mischievous urchin went about trailing ribbons and feathers across people's faces, smartly poking them with stiff quills, even scratching and jabbing them with long pins—what would be done with these offenders?

The imbecile would be shut up as unsafe. The mischievous urchin would be punished; also, I hope, instructed as to the insulting and offensive nature of his behaviour.

We cannot shut up the vast number of women whose hats are thus insulting and offensive. We cannot punish them. But surely they are open to instruction.

Chapter Seven

Decorative Art, Trimmings, and Ornament

THE IMPULSE to decorate the work of one's hands is a human one, not peculiar to either sex. So long as the primitive woman monopolized creative industry, making all the things that were made, she also monopolized decorative art. Hers were the designs in pottery, in basketry, in beadwork, leatherwork, and needlework. But when man began to make things he also felt that racial impulse to adorn his work, and to carve on tool, or weapon, an added ornament.

This human impulse is to be traced in costume, quite aside from the original masculine impulse to increase his impressiveness by external splendors, or the transplanted unnatural appearance of that masculine impulse in the female of our species.

No slightest observation of modern woman's dress can overlook the preponderance of ornament. It is not enough that she be clothed, that her clothing in texture, in color, in pattern, and in craftsmanship shall be, to her mind, beautiful; but she adds to the clothing, decoration; and, still further, to her decorated clothing, she adds distinct articles, not in the least garments, but mere ornaments—or things so considered.

The normal growth of decorative art in textiles is a beautiful study. From simple patterns in weaving to the intricate glories of lace and brocade; from the first crude dyes to the blended loveliness of Oriental rugs; from the earliest variation in stitches to the rich efflorescence of Japanese embroidery, we have a world of interest and true aesthetic pleasure. The evolution of textile art is complex and exquisite; it is also natural, as natural as any pre-human effort of evolution. Lace, for instance, as a separate product, may be traced backward through ever simpler forms, to the crudest beginnings of loose threads, knot work, drawn work and the like. To make the decoration separate and sew it on was a very late step. A bit of rich lace, found among the excavated relics of some lost culture, would prove it one long established.

Since woman was the first, and for all history up to the most recent times, the only worker in textiles, we may so account for her special sensitiveness to beauty in this form. In Japan, where the gorgeous embroidery is made by men, the intense appreciation is also felt, and the embroidered garment also worn, by men. In our race we have just ground for the women's special feeling for fine fabrics, even after they are no longer made by her. The looms of M. Jacquard, the "mules" and "jennys" and all the new machinery which has made man "the spinster" of today, are too recent to have robbed her of hereditary sensitiveness to textile art.[1]

Yet, even after allowing to the full for this special taste of hers, it does not account for such unmeasured indulgence of this taste as allows the decorative quality of an article of clothing, or an accessory to obscure or contradict its use, as in the lace handkerchief.

There are certain laws of decoration, certain principles which govern applied beauty, and woman as a human creature, as a civilized and educated member of modern society, ought to recognize these laws. If a handkerchief was a thing to pin on one's hat as an ornament, or to carry on the end of a stick as a symbol of elegance, then it might be well composed of sheer lace, or of spun glass, or of any light and showy substance. As a piece of cambric used to dry one's—tears, we will say, it has absolute limitations. Not to recognize them is to show one's ignorance of the use of handkerchiefs or of the principles of decoration.

The dress of women, in its unbridled excesses in ornamentation; in its exaggerated pursuance of the motives of delicacy, softness, fineness, and others, plainly exhibits, first, the natural appreciation of textile art and its decorative development; and, second, the lack of true aesthetic training and judgment.

The man's beauty sense, prompting him to personal display as a male, is checked by his judgment as well as by necessity. The woman's, not as gaudy and violent to begin with, is more riotous in expression because necessity does not so directly limit it, and she has, quite apparently, a less effective judgment.

A good illustrative instance is here given. A dressmaker, a woman, made for the approving wear of another woman, this garment. The fabric was a soft fine muslin of a pale yellow tint, covered with a rich pattern of cloudy clustering cherries, in shaded tints of rose, from faint pink to red. In general effect the muslin was beautiful in color; on closer examination it was beautiful in fabric and design. It would seem needless to say that such a material used as a garment should be so cut and arranged as to show all these beauties. The wearer should walk in a rosy cloud, as it were, the delicate tissue sweeping softly as a light veil, floating as the wearer walked. If heavier stuff were needed beneath, the muslin should have flowed freely over it. Here is what the dressmaker made and the proud co-creator and purchaser wore.

The bodice was made as a tight-fitted "five-seam basque," using a thick cream-colored satine as a lining. Such cutting, of course, dislocated the pattern completely, cutting across it in arbitrary lines. It utterly destroyed the effect of the fabric, which might have been a stiff chintz for all the observer knew at a little distance.

The skirt had first a foundation of the same thick satine, stiffened to the knee with a white coarse substance—underneath, of course—and bound with braid. This underpinning hung and moved about as gracefully as if it were made of leather. Upon it the exquisite muslin was arranged in this way: At the back it was bunched together—material perhaps six or seven feet long upholstered in a series of irregular close-set puffs, so as to be fastened to that "back breadth." Down the front and around the hem were a series of alternate rows of "knife-pleatings," fine regular close-set mechanical hard-pressed narrow folds, about four inches deep, first of a cream-colored plain muslin, stiffer than the figured one, but not so stiff as the satine, and then of the soft muslin itself—knife-pleatings of that rich soft cloud of drooping cherries! All up and down the front ran this thatch of pleatings, and four deep around the hem.

Not satisfied with all this industry, there was then brought into the scheme a quantity of—what think you? What would go well with delicate muslin, as a trimming? The beauty of this muslin was so apparent that it visibly needed none; but the dressmaker thought differently. She selected crimson velvet. In the narrow form, as velvet ribbon, it was bobbed and bowed and knotted everywhere, across the bodice, down the front of the skirt, about the sleeves. The collar, I should not forget to say, was a close straight-standing one made of the velvet. But the most conspicuous feature of this masterpiece remains to be mentioned. On either side of that shingled front breadth were "panels" of the crimson velvet—large, long, flat pieces, extending from the belt to the pleated ruffles, two stiff slabs of heavy velvet, sewed onto a skirt of delicate muslin! As a minor detail of artistry I may add that this work of textile torture was accomplished with thread coarse enough to hold suspender buttons. As an instance of the proportion between woman's amount of beauty sense, of the special feminine feeling for fine fabrics, and of the extraneous pressure of the masculine tendency toward gorgeousness; of the desire to exhibit "conspicuous waste" in labor and material, and the brutal irrelevancy of a temporary fashion, I have never known anything better than this murdered muslin.

Of late years we have frequently seen this same insane mixture of discordant motives in what is after all the last epitome of outrage in textile decoration—fur on lace.

Let any woman who has in her head even the crushed and crippled rudiments of artistic feeling study for a few moments what lace is and what fur is.

Lace is the highest, subtlest, most exquisitely delicate of all textile fabrics. It is the slowly evolved product of many ages of loving and intelligent labor. To make it requires a high degree of craftsmanship. To understand, admire and wisely select it shows a high degree of taste. To wear it, appropriately, indicates conditions of sheltered ease and safety, and of high occasion.

Fur is the hide and hair of a beast. It was worn by the cave man, who covered his shivering body with the warm skin of his victims. It is still worn, exclusively, by the Arctic savages, partly because of its saving warmth, partly because they have no other materials at hand. It is also worn by the Russian mujik, for similar reasons—a sheepskin coat is warm, is quickly made, and will wear a long time—without washing.

Fur is the main dependence of savages in all cold countries, and is equally useful to pioneers of any race, though the Shackleton Antarctic expedition, I have understood, found woven flannel goods lighter and warmer.[2]

Fur requires no artistic effort to produce, no dreaming of lovely designs, no sublimated skill in execution. To get fur you only have to kill an animal, tear off his skin, and prepare it.

Fur is at the very bottom of the ladder, the long, long series of steps by which the costume of modern humanity differs from the rude coverings of primitive savagery.

As materials for clothing, that is the difference between fur and lace.

As a matter of artistry, lace is the uttermost margin of decoration. The body must be covered with stronger fabrics, of closer texture; only at the borders, especially where delicate arms and hands appear, or white neck rises like Aphrodite from the foam, are the filmy folds, the snow-crystal patterns of lace appropriate.

To take this ultimate faint border of beauty and fasten upon it a strip of hairy hide is like hanging curbstones along the white tips of a pergola.[3]

Decoration has its laws, like any form of art. When used upon a variety of fabrics it has a variety of forms, but there are principles of truth in each. The exigencies of construction modify somewhat the more severe application of these decorative principles. It is true that embroidery upon the garment as a garment is nobler than when it is applied promiscuously upon the material, and then cut to pieces and sewed together again. It is nobler because it indicates a higher degree of foresight, and because the patterns, so applied, may be more perfectly adapted to the structural limits of the garment.

Nevertheless the application of detached trimmings, while admittedly easier and cheaper, is not in itself offensive if the applied decoration is appropriate.

Our general failure is in perception of what is appropriate; in any keen sense of values and harmonies. As the medieval tailors devised a false method of decoration in "slashes"—cutting totally unnecessary holes in the fabric to arbitrarily exhibit some rich stuff below, so we today cut and trim and tag and button without the faintest conceptions that there are any principles involved.

A woman of high breeding would not mix her speech with slang or indecency; she would note at once a jangle of methods in literature if Mæterlinck suddenly lapsed into the style of O. Henry, or Henry sank to Chambers.[4] She would be pained and shocked at any such discord in music, and contemptuously amused at it if exhibited in setting a table. She would not place a Shaker rocking-chair in a tapestried drawing room, or a yellow cooking bowl among Haviland china. But that same woman will wear lace "trimmed" with fur, and feel no faintest repulsion at the consummate outrage.

We speak of the impropriety of trying to "gild refined gold and paint the lily," but do not notice the impropriety of "trimming lace"—which is itself the lovely ultimate in trimming. Even if the lace were fringed with diamonds it would be a confusion of motives, but to fringe it with fur—!

Charles Reade, with his keen observation and vivid expression of opinion, cried out against the women of his time for spoiling the sheen and flow of silk or velvet by rigid crossing lines of band, ruffle and flounce. He was quite right. Yet beauty-loving woman feels no such objection. I have seen a velvet gown copiously ruffled, narrow curly *velvet* ruffles—about two inches deep.

Velvet, satin, brocade, or any richly patterned fabric, like that tormented cherry muslin, call for little or no decoration. To velvet, in its supreme richness, may be added only the white froth of rich lace, not sewed on as a trimming, but worn at neck and sleeves with the further enhancement of jewels.

Which brings us to another of the main departments of decoration, especially as applied to the dress of women.

The appreciation of shine and color is basic. The smallest child, the lowest savage, even the magpie and the crow, appreciate bright twinkling stones. Those who trade with savages carry beads, which are, to those poor purchasers, jewels. They know nothing of values. They have not reached the "conspicuous expenditure" period. They do not boastfully point out a certain Mrs. Savage as "wearing five hundred thousand dollars' worth of beads." But they do admire jewelry.

The precious stones, valued first for their color and sparkle, then as a permanent form of wealth; and the precious metals, similarly prized; have long been the heart's delight of both men and women. In Oriental races there is no sex-distinction in this matter. The Rajah shines and twinkles with his gemmed turban and ropes of pearls as well as the Ranee.

A beautiful art has grown up in the use of these materials. The goldsmith and silversmith, the carvers of cameo and intaglio, the cunning artificers in jewelry, have added much to the man-made beauty of our life.

We have here many distinct elements of appreciation. First the primal one; color and shine. Second, the sense of value; genuinely prized. Third, added to this last, the ostentatious display of expenditure. Fourth, the artist's love of lovely workmanship.

We, in our modern use of jewels, have reached a stage of sex-distinction wherein this field of decoration is given over almost entirely to women. The man may have:

(a) numbers of scarfpins as valuable as he likes and can afford,
(b) studs and sleeve-links,
(c) a watch-chain or fob,
(d) finger rings.

There he stops, and even in these the element of color and shine is subdued. He may show a refined richness, but the big diamond shirt stud, the blazing ring, are marks of a low taste—for men.

Not so for women. They are given:

(a) brooches and "stick-pins" of all sorts,
(b) necklaces,
(c) bracelets,
(d) tiaras and all hair-ornaments,
(e) earrings,
(f) finger rings,
(g) studs, links, chains, etc.; and furthermore, a multitude of jewelled accessories.

Women are allowed, and happily exhibit, a far larger amount and a far more brilliant kind of jewelry, than men.

Why?

There is one line of approach to this condition, seen among those peasants, or harem beauties, or half-civilized tribes, where the woman carries the family fortune on her person, in silver anklets, or golden sequins.

Another, parallel with this, is the man's desire to enhance both the beauty and the value of his female property. Of two men, the one who can buy, steal, or otherwise secure a beautiful woman all glittering with gems, has accomplished more than the other whose prize does not glitter.

Veblen, in his unforgettable *Theory of the Leisure Class*, clearly shows this motive in all our modern life.[5] While man to-day is denied any conspicuous gorgeousness in his own apparel, he is free to gratify his taste for it vicariously, and his wife, in her clothing and decoration, serves not only to please his eye, but to exhibit his wealth.

It redounds to a man's credit to have his wife well dressed. The better dressed she is, the more expensively dressed she is, the more it redounds. She does not pay for it. It is to his generosity and purchasing power that she owes her splendor.

The third and fourth reasons are even less creditable. Women as dependents are habituated from infancy to receive gifts. They seldom reach the degree of economic dignity which prefers to pay for its own clothing and decoration. There are mingled here two separate feelings; one the natural and harmless pleasure in receiving gifts from loved ones, quite proper in childhood, and to some degree in the adult; the other a sordid eagerness to get them, which belongs only to greedy infancy or frank parasitism.

Boy and girl alike, all small children ask for favors, tease for presents. Boys outgrow it. Girls do not. One would think that a grown woman would be shamed by having people buy things for her, bring her flowers, candy, jewels, she never reciprocating in kind.

Her reciprocation is of another kind, a kind well understood and expected. So long as she lives on gifts, having no purchasing power of her own; so long must she pay—as expected.

Back of all these is another uncomplimentary cause of woman's beaded splendor. She is, in social status, less highly developed than man. By birth always his equal, the conditions of her rearing are grossly unequal. In her dependence, her limited experience, her ruthless restriction to primitive impulses and few forms of expression, it is no wonder that certain low standards of social development survive in her, when her brother, living in a more advanced culture, has outgrown them.

A common instance of this is in that last remnant of adornment by mutilation, the perforated ear. Savages decorate their cattle by slitting ears and dewlaps, splitting or twisting horns, and decorate themselves by tattooing the skin, and by making holes in convenient parts, as ears, lips, noses.

Tattooing still appeals to boys, and to low-class men, earrings are still found on Sicilian sailors; but an educated American man would scorn to make holes in his tissues for decorative purposes. It is true that there is a concession made today in earrings which do not go through the lobe of the ear—only pretend to; our men despise even the pretense. It is high time that our women, in their present rapid development, should give attention to this field of growth as well as others. They do not seem to understand that a certain grade of eagerly expressed masculine admiration, while sweet and stimulating to receive, is quite compatible with an unexpressed masculine contempt for the childishness, the simple savagery, of the creature he is praising.

This savagery, this use of the body itself as a medium of decoration, is shown in that still enduring habit of women, once belonging to the ancient Briton, the naked redman, or African—painting the skin.

The blue-spotted Briton is long out of date; the savage is quite largely civilized, but woman, in the most advanced races, still maintains this early art, and paints her skin.

That she should admire beauty is right; that she should long for it is right; that she should take all legitimate measures to reach a higher standard of beauty is right; but that she should bleach and dye her hair, pencil her eyes, tint her claw-like fingernails, and apply powder and rouge to her skin, is merely a survival of methods so basely primitive that she ought to be ashamed of the taste which can allow them.

It has been stated that the reason why men admire painted women is because it so frankly shows the wish to please, and that the more frankly it shows, the more violently and crudely it is done, the more flattering to masculine vanity is the appeal.

Women have not used their minds upon this matter. Some have reached a stage of social evolution which leaves the powder-puff to the baby-basket and the make-up box to the actress, whose profession demands it; some even have a sort of shrinking from a "painted lady" as if paint meant vice. It does not. It only means a low grade cultural standard.

Those same savages who so painfully and laboriously scarred their poor bodies from head to heel in the effort to be beautiful had no real standard of physical beauty to live up to. So our women, dressed in the most elaborate and expensive "creations," hung with beads and chains and shiny stones, powered white and painted pink, doing their utmost to achieve beauty, are quite unconscious of their own physical shortcomings, or serenely indifferent to them.

If half the effort spent on obtaining beautiful coverings were used to develop a beautiful body to cover, humanity would be lovelier.

There is room for all the richness, delicacy and grace our artistic ingenuity can create, for every lovely fabric, for varied attractiveness in robe and frock; and further for the most exquisite, the most splendid decoration, without committing one of the artistic sins, the savage coarseness, we see so often.

A highly cultivated discriminating taste does not disdain one of the many forms of beauty; in woven fabrics, from the mistiest muslin to the heaviest brocade; in any kind of legitimate decoration or accessory. It admits each "motive"; delights in the art of the jeweler and the lace-maker; in splendor, in variety, but not in misplaced sex-decoration, in a perpetual childishness, or in a grossness of savagery which should have been outgrown thousands of years ago.

As one further instance of this most lamentable feature in woman's dress, we cannot omit their ghastly use of those two primitive materials—furs and feathers.

The exquisite beauty of both, and the added value of warmth, together with the lightness of the bird-covering, make them deservedly popular, both useful and lovely. But the way in which they are used, decoratively, by women, is neither useful nor lovely, but the extreme opposite.

Leaving out for the moment the need of fur garments, where lighter woolen ones would do; and not yet touching upon the ethical or economic questions involved, the point here urged is merely that of decoration.

A woman—a woman of our race, our religion, our standard of college education, our highest culture, thinks it beautiful to fasten on her hat the stuffed corpse of a bird—or many of them. I have seen a woman, charming, interested in settlement work, wearing a hat "decorated" by a close wreath of the stiff little bodies of dead humming birds.[6] Within a few days I passed one, a simple black hat, upon whose front was clapped a flat dead dove; upon the back a second.

This is one degree different from the use of plumage; it adds to the color, the curve, the graceful softness of the feather, quite another matter—the rigid outline of a corpse. Ostrich plumes are lovely. An ostrich, dead, dried, and flattened, is not lovely. Neither is any bird. The beauty of the bird is in its vivid movements, swift and light; its poor carcass is not a decorative "motif" like a fleur-de-lis. Moreover, by so using the corpse, there is instantly brought to the mind of the beholder the painful images of death. They may be inferred from the feathers. They are forced upon us by the cadaver.

Not only in feathers do our women offend, but in fur. Besides the girl's sweet face grins over her shoulder the red jaws of an animal, bead-eyed, white-toothed. It is artificial, of course. It is deliberately made, sold, and worn—as an ornament. Such an object, if it be of a large beast, is terrible. If a small one, and those so used are small, it merely suggests the wholesale slaughter of helpless little creatures, and the most callous indifference to their pain. Their stiff little helpless feet hang down at one end; their grinning little heads, their limply wagging tails, and all this array of ghastliness, is worn as—decoration.

The head-hunters of Borneo hang their houses with the dried skulls of their victims. In ancient South America they kept them, shrunken and blackened, without the skull. But they did not manufacture dead things as ornaments.

Chapter Eight

Humanitarian and Economic Considerations

THE USE of fur and feathers for women's clothing and decoration brings sharply to mind the question of suffering, and of economic loss.

The writer is no ultra-sentimentalist about pain, nor about the taking of life. For the Eskimo to kill animals is necessary if he is to live at all; there is nothing else to eat. Also it is necessary for him to clothe himself in the skins of the animals; there is nothing else to wear. But for a plump woman in New York, who lives in a temperate climate, and who never has to walk more than a few blocks; choosing her own weather at that, if she is well-to-do—for her to wear fur is purely a matter of personal vanity, and of fashion.

That this should be done by coarse-natured, ignorant women; by those too shallow to appreciate any suffering they cannot see; or too hard-hearted to mind it, is not surprising. What is surprising is to see sensitive, refined, intelligent women willing to be accessories to the most prolonged and cruel tortures of harmless animals.

Have they no imagination? Do they deliberately refuse to visualize even once the tragedy that takes place to provide one garment to feed their vanity? Tragedy! It is a dozen, a score, a hundred, if the beasts are small. For an animal to be killed, promptly, by a well-aimed shot, is no great evil. He has no period of terror or of pain. But an animal caught in a steel trap suffers the extremity of physical agony and of blind, limitless terror, for as long as his life can hold out. That this should be done at all can only be defended when human life is at stake, and there is no other way to save it. It is done, for the most part, to provide women with furs.

In climates where furs are needed, men wear them too. In our climate women show their indifference to cold by wearing far thinner clothes than men, and then supplement their inner deficiency by covering their naked shoulders with outer garments of seal and ermine. The woman wears the thin dress, exposes neck and arms, from vanity and fashion. That she bares her own skin, hurts no one; that she demands so many skins of beasts to cover it, hurts terribly; costs a countless yearly toll of agony and death.

The fashion pressure we have not yet discussed; the cruelty and the waste involved come first.

There is hardly a woman who would be indifferent if she walked the northern woods and found a trapped mink staring at her with mad, frightened eyes, jerking his bleeding paw at the end of a taut chain; or a rabbit, hanging in the air by one foot, limp, dislocated, freezing, starving, aching, till he died; or, perhaps worst of all, the thrashed and trampled snow, the grim set trap, and in it the bloody stump of a small paw—gnawed off by the frantic prisoner. Yet these things are going on, in all northern lands, constantly; armies of men tramp the arctic wastes, and snare and trap and kill, kill, kill—in order that women may wear unnecessary furs.

We hear more as to suffering about feathers than about furs; perhaps because the feathers are even more unnecessary. A woman may persuade herself that she "needs" the furs; she can hardly claim necessity for feathers.

There is agony enough in both cases. With the birds there is not the same amount of prolonged torture in traps; but there may be a somewhat greater number of them wounded and escaping to die alone. As to the starving of orphaned young, that happens both to small blind kittens and cubs, and to fledgling birds. It is all bad enough.

The worst pity of it is that it should be done by our women; tender mothers, emotional young girls, sensitive souls that are so grieved to see a horse beaten, a cat stoned, even a poor, staring-eyed mouse caught in one of those merciless wire-spring traps. It is for her that this agony is caused, and not for her need—only for her pleasure.

The savage who wears a necklace of human teeth is not revolted by any thought of the owner's living face, the smiling mouth, from which these teeth were taken. They are glittering white objects—he likes their looks—why go further? There is some serious defect in our education, or "blind spot" in our minds, that we can wear the skins of beasts and never think at all of the little bodies they were torn from.

Would it not be reasonable for every woman of intelligence to determine once and for all, "I will not decorate my body with death trophies. If absolute necessity compel, I will use fur; but not for ornament." Yet, it would be reasonable, but that does not make it probable.

Beyond the appeal to what we call "humane" motives, because human beings are supposed to feel them; comes the economic motive; equally "humane," because only human beings are wise enough to grasp it—and very few of them.

In regard to the fur-bearing animals, there are some of them whose activities are inimical to human interest, that we have to kill in self-defence. In Australia the greatest enemy to mankind is the rabbit. Be it said in his defence that he did not begin it. Some man brought him there; even as some man brought the terrible gypsy moth to this country. But the rabbit in Australia has so multiplied as absolutely to threaten human life by destroying every green thing within his reach. If all trappers would concentrate on Australia for a while and exterminate the rabbit, that would be doing real service to humanity; and our women might dress in rabbit skins without blame. They are warm, they are soft; but quite probably not as "becoming" as seal or otter; certainly not as fashionable.

Veblen's famous law of "conspicuous waste" makes the beast that is rare and hard to get more valuable in our eyes than one near and plentiful; and, as before, we do not reason about it. If Russian sable was as common as rabbit, it would not be considered beautiful.

But after we have killed all the creatures we have to kill, and quite probably utilized their skins to clothe those who need them, every other man who spends his time killing, unnecessarily, is a man wasted.

Human labor is valuable because of its service to humanity. Any human labor which is diverted from that service and spent on what has no value—either in use or beauty—is wasted; and here the dress of women has a large responsibility for economic waste.

At this point we refer only to such parts of the waste as pertain to unnecessary fur and feathers; and proceed now to a very great additional waste, in regard to the latter. As I briefly put it in an earlier article: "The greatest enemies of mankind today are insects. The greatest enemies of insects are birds. The greatest enemies of birds are women. Yet women love birds and hate insects."

Without regard to loving or hating; without regard to pain and fear and slaughter; the point here most seriously urged is the grave economic injury to human prosperity involved in bird destruction.

Agriculture is and must always be the mainstay of our life on earth. As we grow more numerous we shall live more and more by it, for we shall no longer be able to afford great areas of land to turn grass into meat for us, but must support larger numbers from that land by vegetable food.

Besides drouth, which we are learning to counteract by irrigation and dry-farming, agriculture and horticulture suffer most from insects. These tiny forms of life are more dangerous to us today than lions, wolves or tigers. They destroy our food supply, our chief wealth.

In our "struggle for existence" this enemy is today the greatest of all; and to assist us, our chief allies are birds. In a truly intelligent community the fertile fields would be interspersed with trees; not only for food-bearing, shade and beauty, but to provide shelter for birds; for enough birds to keep the fields and orchards free of insect pests.

The farmer's children should grow up to understand and appreciate their "services"; to befriend them, and behind plow, harrow, cultivator and hoe, would hop the grub-destroyer. This is not sentiment; it is sense, good hard economic sense. To save labor, to improve crops, and to make the country more beautiful with shade and musical with song—that is certainly intelligent.

And what do we do?

We kill, kill, kill the birds by millions and millions.

For what?

To put on women's hats. And to make things like gigantic caterpillars for them to wear around their necks.[1]

And why do they do this—the women?

Ah! Why?

Because in the matter of dress women have not yet used their intelligence. They are ignorant of true beauty; ignorant of the suffering caused by their demands; ignorant of the waste involved in supplying them; and indifferent to all these considerations.

* * *

It is impossible to give figures in definite proof of this contention. The Audubon Society supplies much as to the economic value of birds, and the number destroyed.[2] Counting the birds and beasts together, with the time and labor value of the men involved, and the losses to crops as well, it would reach annual millions.

But without any definite lump sum, or any effort to apportion it among women, is not the subject clear enough?

To kill birds in order to wear their feathers is (a) unnecessary; (b) cruel; (c) a waste of time and labor, and (d) an injury to agriculture. No woman able to reason can deny that. Then why take any part in it?

Surely a woman does not have to know that her individual hat trimming cost one hunter's whole day's work, and the labor of all who handled it since, besides the loss of fifty cents' worth of cabbages or corn. She does not need to follow back the five dollars she paid for that flat feathered corpse, to its dwindling returns along the line of those who procured it for her, the farmer standing his loss with no return.

All that is necessary for a human intelligence is to see that the custom of using feathers for hat trimming is *an injury to society*; that ought to be enough.

What right have we to persist in doing what wastes human labor, and increases poverty? If a given act is clearly shown to be socially injurious, those who persist in it should be clearly pointed out as, to that degree, enemies of society. The excuse of ignorance is no longer valid—these facts are commonly known to-day.

But the social conscience of women is not yet as keen as it will be when they realize their citizenship more fully. It is hard to waken a sense of co-responsibility in a subject class; a class not only held in tutelage, but isolated.

We do not yet realize how the individual isolation of women, their close confinement in separate homes, their stringent responsibility to one man, to one family, and complete lack of civic relationships, has weakened the conscience of the world.

The man, in his wide range of duties, has had to be responsible in varied relations; the woman, if she fulfilled her duties to him, and to the children, might ignore all others. But the man is the child of the woman and reared by her. Her limitations invariably limit him.

It is only by understanding these essential restrictions in the whole previous history of women that we may in any way appreciate the paradox of woman's wastefulness and callous cruelty in this matter of personal decoration.

Utterly untrained in the consideration of large social interests;

never taught to think in large numbers, to recognize group-responsibilities; praised first for beauty and then for docility; she has measured her life by the necessity of pleasing those who took care of her. From parents' home to husband's home she moved, never standing free on her own feet, nor dependent on her own resources; and her time, for the most part, was too overfilled with personal duties to her family to leave any room even to speculate as to her duties to the world at large.

The girl child, of course, carries on the decorative tradition of her mother, she is in no position to choose and dictate what she will wear. The young girl has one overmastering necessity upon her, to please, to attract, to command admiration. The married woman is generally either a hard-worked housewife or one of these ornamental domestic pets to whom personal decoration is a life work.

It is rare indeed to find a woman of any age who has ever deliberately considered the question of right dressing and decided for herself what she would or would not wear.

Yet once her conscience, her intelligence, is aroused, she cannot avoid responsibility. Even if she does not pay for the things she wears, she does chose them. Even if she does not design them, does not manufacture them, does not sell them, she does buy them. She is the ultimate consumer; and no blaming of ancestors, no pressure of previous conditions, exonerate the woman of today.

One quick-witted woman, countered, when blamed for wearing feathers on her hat, by saying that she didn't mind killing birds any more than killing the little children who make paper flowers. We are responsible for them, too. Human life is so inextricably inter-knit that none of us can escape our share in the common good or ill. The men who use tobacco are responsible for all that waste of labor, waste of land, waste of life; and, further, for the uncounted loss by fire, caused by their millions of chance-dropped matches.

We are reasoning beings.

We are, to a considerable extent, free agents.

There is no law, natural, civil, or moral, to compel women to bring about this pain and slaughter of other living creatures, this grave injury to humanity. There are for these great wastes and losses "a hundred explanations, but not a single excuse."

* * *

Before approaching the larger economic questions raised by the study of women's dress, more careful attention should be given to points already touched on above; the mistaken theory that there is economic advantage in "furnishing employment," regardless of the use of the work done.

In this matter of unneeded furs, for women, the hundreds, the thousands of men, whose time and labor is spent in killing and skinning animals and in dressing and sewing their skins and in storing and selling those skins—for unnecessary wear—are withdrawn from productive industry. They might as well be making paper flowers—to kindle fires with. The fact that they are paid for doing it, does not make what they do valuable.

We might pay a thousand men to run around in circles, and say that we "furnished employment" to them. That is a fallacy; we furnish exertion—not employment. We give them money, it is true, but they give nothing. Their energy is wasted. This deep-seated and universal delusion about "furnishing employment" blinds us to much cruel waste of time.

The value of a thing in reality is in itself; in its use. If a thing has no real use and no real beauty, is of no service to humanity, then it is not valuable, no matter what may be charged or paid for it.[3]

If all the people on earth spent their time making paper flowers—out of black paper—all our work would be wasted. If half the people on earth did, then half our work would be wasted. If only a million people did it, then the work of a million people would be wasted—no matter what perverted idiots paid them for their black flowers.

I have heard that there are women who make fine silk lace, working with half-numb fingers in rooms over cow-stables for a little warmth—as artificial heat would injure the goods. Others wear out their eyes in fine lace work or embroidery. This is economic waste, a waste of women's lives and energies. Such decoration costs too much; and the fact that some one has money enough to purchase a woman's life, or eyesight, and wear it as trimming, does not make it a human act, or anything but wasteful.

In any living body the economy of nature works steadily along the line of least resistance; always seeking to obtain the most result for the least expenditure of energy. In social life the effort should be the same, and would be, but for the strange interference of our ideas with natural laws.

In order that we may exhibit our ability to pay (again referring to the enunciation of this tendency in Veblen's *Theory of the Leisure Class*), we prefer a garment which visibly requires many days of elaborate toil by expert persons, to one which might be made in far less time, with far less labor. We like to have our clothes exhibit as much labor as possible.

Men, who give attention to dress, choose carefully in materials, and appreciate the skill of the designer, cutter, and finisher. All that is legitimate. So might women select a suitable fabric, a skilled designer, proficient cutters and finishers—and be satisfied.

But they are not satisfied. They delight to point out the delicate refinements achieved by long and close application, enjoying a garment which required the work of six women for a week, better than one which could be made by two in a day.

And all this they justify on the ground that these workers are paid for doing it; that the purchaser has "furnished employment" to them. Yet those same patrons of dressmakers, if they are also patrons of art; if, that is, they have any knowledge of value in painting, know enough to condemn the niggling assiduity that putters forever over the canvas, and to admire most that firm perfection of technique which knows perfectly what it wishes to do, and does it in one stroke.

These questions of economic value are confusing mainly because they deal with large numbers; and also, of course, because of the various profound misconceptions already in our minds. If one starts freshly, with a simple problem in small numbers and restricted space, it is not so hard.

Suppose, for instance, you have one person on an island for life. His economic advantage surely lies in producing from that island the most wealth with the least labor. Or suppose you have a group of one hundred people confined to one hundred square miles of land, and cut off from all other connection with humanity. The economic advantage of these people, as is visible to a child, lies in producing from that land the most wealth with the least labor—food, clothing, shelter, furnishings, all manner of things of use and beauty.

Suppose one person in some mysterious way, has power over all the others, to make them work; either power by slavery, or power by holding all the supplies on which they lived, or its equivalent—money.

Now suppose this person used this power to promote the activity of the others, so that they should, without injury, make more and better and lovelier things; then that group would be richer. Even if the master kept all the things, except what the workers needed to live on, still the sum of wealth would be increased.

But if this man had a fancy for soap bubbles, and kept half of the workers busy making soap bubbles—in place of food, clothing, etc.—

he would reduce the wealth of the group by half. Now see! He might quite fairly and fully pay them for making bubbles, but he would only have to pay them with what the other half made. The real "goods" of the country would be reduced, and, if they had money, it would only buy half as much; the cost of living would go up mightily, on account of the bubbles.

The more people who were hired to blow bubbles, the less would be the wealth of the group; and the more expensive would be every necessity of life.

Yet the master, gratifying a refined, aesthetic taste by this iridescent cloud of bubbles floating in the air, rolling on the grass, twinkling and bounding everywhere; and handing out the pay envelopes every Saturday night, might perfectly well defend his position on the ground that bubbles were beautiful and that he had paid for them—he "furnished employment" to half the population.

Now if the whole world of us were properly clothed, as well as fed, housed, warmed, taught, and so on; if all real human needs were met and there was plenty of leisure time left; if there were people who for the pure pleasure of doing lingerie over a gown and added a fantastic richness of embroidery, that would be no loss. There is room and to spare for the extra beautifying of garments—after one have garments enough. But the present contrast between the woman with a thousand dollars spent upon her clothing alone, and twice that in ornament; and the woman who has not enough to be clean and warm—this contrast indicates a very low state in either humanitarianism or economics or both.

We cannot, in one generation, bridge the gulf which has been centuries in the making. We can neither give our cloaks to the beggars nor eliminate the beggars—in a moment. But we can begin to relate our own problems to the world problem, and to grasp the principles involved.

A human being, man or woman, should seek to wear clothing which caused no needless pain or loss, either to bird, beast, or human being; and which has for economic merit that lasting test—the most achievement for the least expenditure.

Some one, not unusually short-sighted, may ask: "But if these men are not killing birds and beasts for use, they will be thrown out of employment. What will they do? They will starve." No, they will not starve. They will merely, finding that there is no more market for those wares, turn their attention to other work. They will have to.

There are people "thrown out of employment" every time a fashion changes. When "Irish lace" is "in," the makers of Valenciennes must suffer.[4] When beads are "out," there will be mourning in the glass works. Indeed, in merely catering to our seasonal demands, there are thousands and thousands "thrown out of employment" every year. We need not muster up any sudden sympathy for the trappers. They can trap enough to eat till they find a better job.

The elimination of fur and feathers from the yearly demand would reduce the expense account of women's clothing most materially. Only lace and jewels remain as conspicuous means to exhibit wealth.

There is no reason, no real reason, that is, why women spend as much as they do on dress. Quite aside from the ultra extravagant ones, there is a most unnecessary drain on ordinary purses for this use.

Some thirty years ago it was estimated that a woman could dress well enough to be in good society, on $300 a year. This allowed for one new evening gown, and one new tailor suit each year, both lasting over as second-best for another; and may be filled out according to preference. It might have been as follows:

Evening dress	$75.00
Evening wrap (per year)	15.00
Gloves, fans, etc.	15.00
Hats	40.00
Tailor suit	50.00
Shoes	15.00
Hose	6.00
Summer dresses	20.00
Handkerchiefs	4.00
Coats, per year	15.00
Blouses, neckwear, etc.	30.00
Underwear	15.00
	$300.00

Even at that time I can remember these estimates being scoffed at as ridiculously low by a group of trained nurses. Yet one would hardly imagine a trained nurse as needing more than that list, substituting her starched uniforms for the richer evening wear.

Of course we must bear in mind, when criticizing women's expenditure for dress, that it is to them not only clothing, not only decoration, not only an avenue for their restricted personal expression;

but that it has a distinct strategic value. It is often the means of securing a livelihood. A dress, even a hat, may turn the scale of attractiveness and secure the attention of a supporter-for-life. We cannot call the most extravagant costume wasteful, if, by means of it, a whole life of ease is secured.

But we can and should discriminate between such frankly stated values as this, and the unacknowledged tendency urging women to spend and spend, even after they have accomplished that main purpose.

Chapter Nine

Larger Economic Considerations

IT IS possible for a man to spend a good deal of money on his clothes. Some men do. Socks and underwear may be of silk; shoes made to measure; the most expensive tailors patronized; and all purchased in profusion and with continual variety. But item for item and change for change, the woman can out spend him, and add an endless list of articles he cannot parallel.

While it is still possible, with intelligent care, for a woman to dress on three to five hundred dollars a year, to say nothing of the millions who do it on fifty or less; the woman who is "in society" finds three to five thousand a moderate allowance, and many spend more. The influence of this down-reaching example spreads far and wide, to all classes of society; an insidious pressure upon all to spend and still to spend, on clothes.

Here we come nearer to that governing force called Fashion; but, postponing as long as possible; supposing, for the moment, that our costumes remained the same in style; we will consider merely their profusion and elaboration, as instances of economic waste.

If we had one unvarying kind of dress, as with the Chinese, it would be easily possible to have the necessary minimum, and then to allow a generous margin for personal variation in taste. The minimum in clothing rests on those basic principles mentioned in previous chapters; we must be covered, we must be kept warm, we must be adorned, we must be properly expressed—in legitimate symbolism. This calls for garments of such and such size, color, shape, durability, and decoration.

The "irreducible minimum" would be like the classic instance of Mr. Fox, the father of The Society of Friends, who, wishing to remove the subject of dress entirely from his mind, had a suit of leather made for him, put it on, and retired to the woods to meditate undisturbed.[1]

Without trying to indicate any one permanent garment such as this, it remains perfectly possible for man or woman to settle on some kind of costume as necessary and fitting; to allow what is necessary to provide it; and to limit their expense for dress to that amount.

Throughout the country there are women in plenty, who from economic necessity, do precisely this as far as the amount goes; but are not thereby freed from anxiety and discontent. Because of the continuous extravagance and display of those whose main business in life is to wear clothes; because of the catering of all the shops to this level of extravagance; because of the deeply rooted sentiment among men as well as women in regard to what is admirable in feminine attire; the steady influence upon all women is to spend more than is necessary, or to wish to even if they cannot.

The general result, as here suggested, is that more people work in textile manufacture than are necessary; that more people work in the construction and decoration of garments than are necessary; that more people work in the distributing and selling of garments than are necessary; and that the purchaser spends not only more money, but more time, thought, and emotion than is necessary.

The evolving of these super-physical tissues is a social process, and should be as normal, as pleasant, as other legitimate social processes. The arts and crafts involved are interesting and not injurious if properly organized. To shear the sheep, to wash and card and dye the wool, to spin and weave, to cut and sew—these are not "dangerous trades," or need not be. And if all this was rightly done, we should have a certain regular number of workers in these trades, all carefully educated to know the use and value of the work, the whole history of each craft and its relation to the others.

In proportion to the population, with full allowance for a margin of fluctuating taste and demand, we ought long since to have determined what proportion of human labor is necessary to clothe humanity. There is a norm for all proportionate social functions; and there is the same liability to the abnormal, to morbid monstrous growth and to disease, that is found in physical functions. The physical body spends a certain amount of its energy in producing hair. If too much goes to hair there is less for other use. A woman with five yards of heavy hair would be a freak, not a beauty. A man with whiskers he could step on would not find them an advantage or an ornament.

There is a legitimate limit to society's output of clothing.

Reduced to the work of one person, alone and wholly self-dependent, the more time spent on making garments, the less for securing food, shelter, or any other advantage. In a small group, say of twenty, similarly restricted, two might produce and one prepare and serve the food; four more do laundry work and all cleaning; four build the shelter and the furniture; other four make all dishes, utensils, tools and the like; and there would remain four for clothing and every other kind of work. All these should enjoy short hours and hold equal value and honor in the community.

With our present organization of mills and of labor the year's work of one man would clothe thousands. Our vast improvement in machinery and applied force has reduced, or should have reduced, the number of workers and the hours of labor. That it has not is due to more than one economic error, but among them there is no escaping this simple fact: if we wear twice as much clothing as we need the people who make it have to work twice as long. Waste is waste, whether it applies to the labor of one person or of a million. Waste is waste whether it is paid for or not; that is the point we have to understand.

Think again of the simple facts in an individual case of self-supplying labor; following nature's guide—the line of least resistance. It is good for the individual to work, i.e., to expend energy, to an amount sufficient to use and develop his powers; not to over-use and exhaust them. It is good for the individual to supply his more primitive needs easily and quickly in order that he may apply his energy along lines of higher development.

If, as in savagery, the whole time and energy of the race is spent in the effort to obtain food and shelter, no further progress can be made. The reason that keeping cattle is a social advantage over hunting is that it provided more food with less exertion—man had time to think. The reason that agriculture is a still greater advantage, the base of all our higher growth, is that through its generous supply the labor of a few people could feed many—and then the others were free to do other things. Thus alone have we have been enabled to develop our wide variety of arts, crafts, trades and professions.

In order to develop the highest social traits we must have a degree of leisure. So far we have made our halting and uncertain progress by striving for these social benefits separately as individuals, or establishing them within limits, as classes. But the irresistible progress of democracy makes it continually clearer that among "fellow citizens" where "the majority rules," it is necessary to raise the standard of that majority.

A despotism, an oligarchy, an aristocracy, an hierarchy, may subsist on a sub-stratum of overworked, underpaid, ignorant "subjects." But democracy, which in its largest sense means the full awakening and inter-relating of all the people, the awakening of society to conscious life—this calls for intelligence, for education, for good manners and morals in everybody—no less.

We in America, vaguely recognizing this, have striven to offer free schooling to all, and to provide free libraries, museums, and other sources of education. But we have not yet seen that a population working ten or twelve hours a day at uncongenial toil; mechanical, over-specialized, unrelated, in which the worker takes no interest, cannot be intelligent, educated, or well-bred. Until each citizen has the opportunity for the fullest personal development, our democracy is and must be inferior.

Can we not see at once that if all our people were of the lowest grade we now endure we should have no standing as a nation? Can we not see farther that the greater the proportion of wise, well-developed, well-educated, healthy and happy people, the higher stands our country among the nations? Can we not think far enough to see that by every one of the work-dulled, work-wearied, work-embittered population, we and Our Country are lowered, weakened, checked?

Whether we see it or not, it is so; and in relation to the subject of this book, we should recognize also that the clothing industries constitute too large a share in the overwork of the population.

There is the initial expense for cotton, wool, flax, silk; the necessary amount of labor to raise as much as we need; and the unnecessary amount, the waste of time, of strength, of skill, of land also, used to supply the materials we do not need. Then all the mills and shops and workrooms where the successive processes go on to fit the materials for our use—or our waste; all the machinery of transportation with its fuel; all the warehouses, stores and shops, and their thousands upon thousands of foot-sore employees.

If the women of today use up twice as much dress goods as they need, then they are responsible for wasting half the labor of all those toiling millions.

Even if we paid as much money as we do now for our clothing, and used but half as much, the saving in time alone would lift the standard of living for all those who work to furnish us with garments.

As a minor part of this view some consideration should be paid to the time spent by the consumer. Freely admitting that there are women so besotted with personal decoration and its complex materials that they actually enjoy spending hours, days, weeks, months, discussing, studying, examining, purchasing, and in all the time-devouring struggles with the dressmaker, it remains true that there are other women who do not enjoy it. Even if we were all exquisitely trained in the understanding and appreciation of textile art, and of design and execution in costume, but a few would care to devote so much time to it. As it is, while undeniably it gives pleasure to some, it is a weariness, a bore, a real burden, to others.

Our standards of femininity are such that we condone, even admire, in a woman, this incessant concern about the details of costume, where we despise and condemn it in a man. To see a group of men immersed in a discussion of "trouserings" and the like, we find pitiable; some day we shall learn that it is not only as much, but more pitiable, in women. Remember always that the instinct of sex-decoration is primarily male, and all the intense prepossession shown in it by women is a proof of their abnormal position. In a well-ordered civilization the women would long since have evolved a suitable costume; useful, beautiful, economical, allowing for full personal expression; and if there was any difference in the interest shown by the two sexes in their personal appearance the excess would be on the part of men, not women.

In our present condition we find each woman carrying among her other handicaps this: that she must spend more on dress than a man; more in time, thought, labor, or money—sometimes in all. She is required to dress in a certain manner on pain of more kinds of loss than threaten him. Even in the lowest grades of hard work, of dirty work, she is expected to be "neat" in her appearance where he is not; she must add to her other labors the extra toil of keeping her clothes clean—and his as well.

Let us now see the effect on men of this general waste in dress.

The boy, first impressed by the difference in clothes between his sister and himself—that totally unnecessary and most injurious distinction—early learns to despise "girl's clothes." But because they are "girl's clothes," used as a sex-distinction and a sex attraction from the first, as for instance in the broad flaunting ribbon fastened to the hair of the little girl, to cry aloud as far as it can be seen: "Girl! Pretty!"; as soon as the boy reaches "the impressionable age" he begins to be attracted by, instead of despising, girl's clothes.

An illustration in a current magazine presents, all by itself, as if seen in a window exhibit, what is described as "a meltingly feminine slipper." The meltingly masculine heart seems always particularly susceptible to slippers—see Cinderella. But whatever the foolishness is, the "frou-frou," the "tap of little heels," the glint of jewels or bright silk, the man is attracted by the clothes.

He does not object. He does not criticize. He expects her to dress to attract him, and ignores her if she does not; even sharply condemns her if she seems indifferent to his opinion and wears what he considers "queer." When he loves her he faces, even with ardor, the privilege of providing her with those "feminine attributes," as was ingenuously shown by *The Little Minister.*[2] In the matter of gifts, beyond the flowers and sweetmeats which have become a convention, he bestows bonnets, furs, and, always, jewels. Think for a moment of how different the relation of the sexes would be, even in this one particular, if women were independent. Suppose they wore neat, comfortable, beautiful and becoming clothes; restrained and simple; human rather than feminine, and *provided them for themselves*. Suppose it was no more allowable for a man to propitiate a woman by spending money for some article of clothing, than for her to reverse the process, and try to propitiate him by buying him a new hat, or a fur overcoat. It is a stretch, of the imagination, I admit—but try it. Try to imagine women as frankly offended if anyone tried to buy their favor—to bribe them.

Then what would a man do who wanted to please a woman? He would have to please her by his actions—not his gifts. He would have to *be* what she liked, instead of giving her what she liked, which is easier far. In their purchaseability women surrender that deep-rooted power of race improvement which is theirs by nature.

If women were true to their real place and duty they would steadily lift the world by demanding a higher standard of character and conduct in men; whereas, as it is, they steadily hold back the world by demanding a higher standard of expense.

The man must "support" the woman; and this not only in the early sense of providing a shelter, food, and warmth; but in an ever-increasing limitless sense of providing for her unmeasured wants in clothing. He must provide for his wife and his children not only necessaries, comforts, and, if he can, luxuries, but he must add to that a load of expense for things neither necessary, comfortable, nor luxurious—merely demanded by girls and women as parts of their costume, or accessories thereto.

This anticipated burden is a considerable factor in postponing marriage. This is what the father has in mind when he looks from his highly decorated, excessively attractive daughter to the young man who wants to marry her, and says: "Can you support her, my boy?"

The man who has to support the over-dressed wife, and later, the over-dressed daughters, must needs acquire more money than would otherwise be necessary. It does not enable him to earn more. His own market value is not increased by the demands made upon him; often it is decreased, from mere anxiety. But get the money he must; and in many cases he does.

The tremendous tension of our economic life is by no means all due to any one cause, but among many this is no inconsiderable one. It works in the proverbial "vicious circle." The woman, placed in her unnatural position of dependence upon the man, is forthwith obliged to develop new powers of attraction in order to catch and hold him. Where in the natural relation he had to manifest all the splendor possible in order to please her, she now reverses the natural process and caters to him.

Since his taste is simple and narrow, asking always for one thing, sex-attraction, she develops sex-attraction to a fine art. Since there are limits to personal beauty and drawing power, but practically none to the extra-personal additions of clothing and ornament, she launches out on a boundless, soundless sea of extraneous adornment, of a superficial, extensible femininity. And since man's taste is nothing if not variable; while the inexorable laws of social advantage have given us a permanent monogamy, the play of other laws have added to "the one woman"—liable to become monotonous—the infinite variety of a thousand costumes.

With this foundation lying broad and deep beneath, the superstructure rises accordingly.[3] To please the man the woman must "dress."

Out of long habit and associative advantage she develops an "instinct" for such decoration. To please the woman the man caters to this instinct developed to please him, and buys for the woman the ornaments wherewith she maintains her hold upon him.

A whole literature has grown up around this inverted custom. The poets have aided it. The artists have aided it; seldom the sculptors. That grave and noble art must bear in mind the beauty of form alone, and of all costumes shown in sculpture that is the most beautiful of which there is least, or which least conceals the Real Beauty—that of the body itself. The painter may delight in shadowy velvet, or the curving sheen of satin, and in every joy of harmony or contrast in color. The sculptor loves the rounded lines and interplay of bone and muscle, the grace and proportion of the whole body.

But sculpture has practically no influence upon the dress of women. We decorate our parlors with casts of great statues, and sit unabashed before them, dressed like dolls and dummies.

Think for a moment of any other animal, preserving statues of its normal shape—and living on amid such statues in distorted, crippled travesty of its own true form!

But the condition is here. Man's admiration for woman is so completely clothed and ornamented that there have even arisen those weird forms of unnatural gratification in which the garments arouse sensations not kindled by the body itself.

So the vicious circle goes on.

Men are taxed heavily to provide the decorations of women. Women, to please men, must have those decorations. Other men, to obtain the money to decorate their women, turn all their energies to catering to the ever-growing taste for these attractions.

When we criticize, as well we may, the gross appeal only too evident in many of our women's garments, let us not forget while we blame the women who wear them, that the articles were designed by men. They knew what taste to please.

Can we, by another stretch of the imagination, conceive of disinterested artists designing simple, noble, lovely garments; and with one more effort, of women wise enough to choose those beautiful things? Even then, the women so attired would be at a disadvantage compared with those whose unerring sense of sexuo-economic gain led them to put on things not indeed beautiful, but efficaciously "attractive."

It is cost added to cost, always more ingenuity, more daring and flagrant attempts, more expense; and the women, some knowingly, but more unknowingly, lending themselves to this evil process of social debasement.

The economic loss is widespread; it is both open and insidious. It appears in the enormous figures of direct expense among the wealthy, and the even worse extravagance of the merely vicious. It weighs on the worthy man who is legally supporting "good" women, and also on the unworthy man who is illegally supporting "bad" ones.[4]

But it goes farther than that. It reaches down the whole line of workers; all who manufacture, handle, sell these things. It changes the habits of a whole people; weakens the power of self-denial; develops over-indulgence on other lines—on all lines.

Just as a disease in one part of the body must needs involve other parts, so any social malformation or excess affects the body politic throughout.

Our moralists and economists of past times have not been slow to blame what they were content to call "feminine vanity" and "the extravagance of women" as if that was the whole story. But neither men nor women have realized the misplacement which is the cause of all this evil; that morbid relation between man and woman which by making him her food supply has made general discord of what should be general harmony.

It is not a permanent condition. It is not a natural condition. It may been seen changing under our eyes today, in proportion as women become economically independent. A girl, easily able to supply her own needs, is not so dependent on presents. A woman who still pays her own bills, though married, can love her husband disinterestedly—for his character and achievement, regardless of his purchasing power. A mother, still paying her own bills and wishing to help provide for her children, is not likely to spend more on clothing than is necessary. And at any age, if she is taught from infancy to recognize, to love and honor, real human beauty, she will have too much respect for that highest form of life to dress it like a monkey or a paper doll.

Such a change in woman would work an equal change in man. Brought up in affectionate equality, little girls and boys dressing and playing similarly, he would not learn that precocious contempt for one who is "only a girl." If she were agile, muscular, free-limbed, well-trained and vigorous; if her clothes were those proper to agile youth, beautiful in line and color, in texture and make, but not supersexual in any way; then the attraction between young men and women would be natural and not fostered artificially.

In *Consuelo,*[5] when the heroine, fleeing through the mountains with a young shepherd, puts on a shepherd's costume for safety and convenience, the youth naively admits that his feelings toward her instantly changed—that he found it easy to be her friend and comrade merely, where before he had been passionately attracted.

It is not necessary that the dress of men and women be identical. It is not by any means necessary for us to give up variety and beauty, delicacy and ornament. But the beauty and delicacy, the decoration and variety, should be along lines of real textile construction and personal feeling—not along these obvious lines of sex-attraction.

In direct influence on our economic conditions this would tend to greatly simplify life and reduce expenses; to shorten hours of labor; to lessen the strain and pressure on hard-worked men of all classes, and to greatly elevate what we may call the *economic morals* of women.

There would appear a new standard of taste. Of two garments, equally good, we should learn to be proudest of the one costing the least labor in manufacture, and also the least labor to keep clean. Instead of the frivolous variable taste, never clear as to what it wants, buying continuously and without satisfaction, we should develop a pleasant certainty as to what we wanted; select with definite judgment, and enjoy for years thereafter.

The reactive results on the whole economic field would reach far wider than can be indicated here. Women are half the world and of the strongest formative influence on the other half. If women reached a sound economic basis of thought on this one subject it could not fail to affect the judgment of the whole world.

And from the lives of all women who work, who think, who already long for beauty and comfort and peace of mind in clothing, there would be lifted an enormous burden. Also from the lives of many million men.

Chapter Ten

The Force Called Fashion

IF WE SAW a million people, moved by some invisible power, rise from their seats and bow to the ground at the same hour each day, we should attribute this act to a religious belief.

If we saw them all suddenly change their diet from meat to fish, or from fish to vegetables, we should attribute it to some hygienic conviction, if there was no change in the available food supply. If the change in attitude, or the change in diet, was repeated indefinitely; the prostrations and genuflections varying from kneeling to jumping, from dancing to lying prone; or if we saw the dietary scheme alter from year to year, from month to month—then we should be forced to consider that in religion and hygiene these people had no real convictions, no settled faith or established facts on which to base their conduct.

In the matter of clothing, which, as may be seen on the most casual study, is of the most vital importance to humanity, there is some mysterious and compelling power at work, which forces people by millions and millions to wear clothing which they neither like, admire, or need; in which they are not comfortable, and which they cannot afford.

So heavy is the pressure of this force that many heroic persons engaged in great work for the world's good, and quite conscious of the evils of our methods of dressing, have deliberately given up the effort to decide on their own clothing, both as too difficult, and as so costly in the opposition and opprobrium excited by any efforts at freedom as to imperil the other work in which they were interested.

We have, half in earnest, personified this force; we speak of "Dame Fashion," of "Fashion's Mandates," or say "Fashion's Decrees" with all the solemnity of one naming his hereditary monarch or tutelary deity. Yet none of us really imagines that there is any extra-human power at work upon us in this way. We know, or may know, easily enough, that our conduct is the result of (a) heredity; (b) environment; and (c) the individual will. This last factor is open to pressure, both from within, from the knowledge, the ideas and convictions of the individual; and from without, in some form of persuasion or coercion from others.

Since human beings do not exist singly, and since artificial isolation instantly produces morbid reactions, we cannot make any study of absolutely individual choice in clothing. Further, as we have seen, clothing is essentially a social product, and must be so discussed.

Our question in regard to Fashion is not so much: "Why do *you* wear something so foolish, so ugly, so utterly injurious as high heels?" but "Why do *we* do it?"

The first answer is generally one based on economics. In our stage of sociologic discussion, with the Socialist doctrine of economic determination so widely known, it takes little thinking to discover the economic factor in almost any human performance. A little more thinking easily shows that there are others, many others, also effective.

If we go deep enough, examining this power of fashion in other instances, we shall easily find it at work in cases where it would puzzle Marx himself to show economic pressure, as for instance in the unanimous swing of young boys toward marbles in March.[1]

Among children, or those sociological children, savages, we find this pressure well-nigh absolute. The power of custom, the demand for absolute conformity, is seen to be stronger as we go backward in social progress. The lower the stage of social development the more rare is individual freedom, the more difficult, the more dangerous—a fact clearly expressed by the formula: "Specialization is in proportion to organization." Those who prize their "individuality," and who fear that advancing Socialism will reduce or injure it, should carefully study this fact. It is only in high social relation that any full and perfect individuality is possible.

Thus we have one factor in the power of fashion explained without reference to economics; it is the tendency to conform, common to primitive humanity, and based mainly on the psychic characteristic of imitation, common to us and monkeys. Also there is the objection of the mass to the freedom of the individual. There is no question about this, even in modern and comparatively intelligent life. Let any individual deliberately choose to be "different" in no matter how small an instance, and from the intimate criticism of the family and the faithful wounds of a friend, to the general disapproval of the public, the painful consequences must be borne.

Little by little humanity has burst its chains in some lines of action, notably in the useful arts. Every step of improvement in tool, weapon, or machine, involved doing something "different," and every step was met by the same objection, criticism, resistance. Nevertheless the growing-power, which is as clearly seen in the evolution of society as in that of earlier life-forms, has made us sprout and push with new inventions, and, in the more practical lines, where advantage was clear and easily proved, we have progressed.

Those who are so fond of extolling the merits of conservatism, calling it "the balance wheel," "the necessary brake," and other pleasant names, should face the bald fact that every single advantage we have over the cave man has come by doing something different, something new, and that every single advantage has invariably been opposed by the beneficent conservatives.

The predominant human traits distinguishing us from all other animals, civilized man from savage, and grown persons from children, are the Reasoning Power and the Applied Will. To be able to think, judge, decide for oneself, and to have the force of character to act on one's decision—these are the supreme human characteristics. Not love itself is able to maintain life, much less promote its growth, without these faculties of self-judgment and determined action.

In view of this it becomes highly important to find in our modern life any department wherein these higher faculties are not used; and where, on the contrary, the primitive attitude of conformity is maintained under penalty.

The economic agencies working to keep up the rapid fire change of fashion are easy to see. The largest is the pressure from the manufacturers and dealers, with all the designers, tailors and dressmakers. It is obvious that the necessary clothing of a human being would not begin to "furnish employment" to the multitudes now occupied in making and selling unnecessary, poor and ugly clothing. All this force of workers, subsidizing the press by their advertisements, continually operates to create and maintain a "forced draught" of changes in costumes, and this obvious fact, to some minds, quite accounts for the kaleidoscope. But it is not nearly enough. There is further required an explanation of two things: First, to what appetites, natural or artificial, does this effort appeal? Second, what is it which prevents the counteraction of the Judgment and the Will?

Let us suppose that a vast group of capitalists and workers found a continuous profit in making and selling colored ear-muffs, to be changed each week. How could they make us buy those ear-muffs—if we did not want them? How could they make us change the color every week—if we did not wish to?

The economic pressure actuating the producer is clear enough, but what is the pressure actuating the consumer? Admitting the "tendency to conform," the question still arises as to how we induce the "leaders of fashion" to change—in order that the others may conform as rapidly as possible?

Here we have three lines of approach: one the economic dependence of women upon men, which, as we have shown, causes her to vary in costume in order to win and hold his variable taste; another the tendency to "conspicuous expenditure," shown by Veblen, which causes both men and women to exhibit clothes, rather than wear them—the more the better; and third, a result of our artificial classification of society, in which social position is indicated by dress, with the consequence that the natural tendency to conform and to imitate is reinforced by the desire to resemble someone higher up, a species of "protective mimicry."

That the clothing of women is more open to variation than that of men, in spite of all efforts of producers to work off their wares on both sexes, is due to several causes. There is the main distinction of their lives, that men as a class make and hold their positions by what they do rather than by what they look like; the greater standardization of men's clothes, with its flat and determined symbolism in uniform; the fact that men please women not by elaborate changes of costume but by personal qualities and the whole range of gift and bribes; and, further, that the activities of men call for the exercise of individual judgment and will more than those of women.

In the matter of conformity there is little to choose. Men have swallowed their dose wholesale, they are far more alike in appearance than women, and it is even more difficult to make them show personal peculiarity in dress. Moreover the man's dress, with all its limitations, is far nearer to the needs of the real basis, the human body. He must have freedom of movement, he must have some power and skill. He could not, conceivably, be made to wear anything that crippled him in action, like the "hobbleskirt," or the stilt heel.

But the woman, unfortunately, is open to every pressure that can be brought to bear—economic, sexuo-economic, what she calls "social," and all the others, major and minor, and against these she has not yet learned to present the solid front of reason, knowledge, artistic taste, or personal judgment.

She makes no resistance at all.

A sadder, more pitiful, more contemptible spectacle it would be hard to exhibit, than these millions of full-grown human creatures hurriedly and continuously arranging and rearranging their hair, their clothes, their hats, their shoes, their very fingernails—because someone has so ordered.

There is not a murmur of resistance, not a moment of criticism.

"This is beautiful! Wear it!" says the Power, and by millions and millions they agree: "This is beautiful!"—and wear it. In a few years, a few months, they laugh at it and say: "It is not beautiful! How could we wear it!" Yet never once do they hesitate to accept the next proclamation.

One would think that in members of a freeborn race, in a free country, with all our traditional admiration of revolution, our women would cringe in shame to be so harried and driven by masters they cannot even name. One would think they would lift their heads and say, "Why must I?—I will *not!*" But no, they bow their heads all one way, like river grass streaming in the current, and over them, their lives long, flows this stream of clothing and decoration. They do not oppose it, being apparently will-less in the matter. So long, so complete, so unbroken has been their surrender that it does not, in all their lives, cross the minds of most women that it would be possible for them to wear what they personally preferred. They have no preference. They have not taste. They have no standards, ethic, economic, hygienic, or artistic, whereby to measure and criticize the things poured upon them. On the contrary, they have deified the power that governs them, and worship it. They call it—"Style."

There is a mystic cult in this worship. It is approached with a special air; it cannot be described in words; it is supposed to convey some indefinable merit and superiority on its exponents and devotees. Being ruthlessly analyzed by those who do not readily bow down to mysteries, it seems to consist in discerning the distinctive note in the newest fashion, and harmonizing the costume to that note. This is perhaps better than wearing a jarring hodge-podge of various "notes," or a subdued failure to catch any of them, but it confers no merit on the "note" itself. The crinoline was just as ugly, clumsy, and silly on the most buoyant balloon-lady of them all; the "Grecian bend" as insulting to all beauty; the "tied-back" of the eighties, and "hobble-skirt" of yesterday as ignominiously crippling. To successfully and harmoniously carry out a design of utter folly is no high ambition.

Yet our women, practically all of them, yearn their lives long for "style"; strive for it, study it, admire it, envy it, seek to buy it at any price. Those who attain it bask in a complacency so absolute that one rubs one's eyes to be sure that so much satisfaction is attained on so fragile and uncertain a basis. For this so-worshipped "style" is not something to be attained by the use of the intellect, by strength or skill or patience. The ability to discern in the tossing flood of ceaseless changes this mystic line of superiority, and seize upon it, requires, it would appear, a peculiar cast of mind. So vague and indefinite is this gift, that even its possession is attested only by the opinions of other persons—and they, alas, disagree. This, that, or the other woman, among the trooping, eager, subservient masses, is hailed as a high exponent of style—by some. Others deny it. None can explain or prove either affirmation or denial. When pursued to its sources in the mind we find a singular psychologic background.

Following the life of an individual, we see the girl-child first influenced by sex-distinction in dress, the things "proper to little girls" as quite distinct from things "proper to little boys." The baby has, of course, no choice in dress, though quite open to its influence. What moulds the mother's choice?

It is a long way back, counting from egg to hen, and from hen to egg, but one strong influence modifying our taste in dress is the habit of playing with dolls. The girl child is given dolls, and, partly by instinct, mainly by imitation, repeats maternal cares and labors. The child pets and punishes, feeds and dresses her dummy infant as she sees her mother do to the real one; and the mother in turn pets and punishes, feeds and dresses her real infant, as she did when a child to her doll.

Where maternal conduct is so largely a matter of "instinct" we need not be surprised to see the child's conduct so closely resemble the mother's, and the mother's resembles the child's.

The child, given a bundle of odds and ends as gay as possible, her "doll rags," proceeds to the best of her ability to adorn the body of her favorite. A childish taste is to be expected—in children; and where it never grows wiser, never is educated, never is refined by the study of beauty, nor strengthened and clarified by a knowledge of natural and aesthetic love, it remains childish through life.

The similarity in taste between children, savages, and women is sufficiently marked to be noticeable, as we have seen in the study of decoration. It should be outgrown by the use of progressive intelligence, and by education; but neither is used in the clothing of women. The child gets her start in taste as a doll-dressed baby, and develops it on her baby-dressed dolls. She then, among her young associates, comes under the influence of that strong human tendency, imitation.

Children are as helplessly and as ruthlessly imitative as savages. They long to wear what the others wear; they cruelly criticize and ridicule the hapless child who forms any exception to the rule. Boys are as subject to this force as girls, their superiority in clothing is related to their status—not their sex.

One would think that parents and teachers might combat this primitive tendency to imitate; might explain that an article of clothing was to be judged on its merits, by its intrinsic or applied beauty, its use, its power of expression. One would think that it might be shown to any intelligent child of eight years that a hundred thousand ugly hats or silly ribbons were no *less* ugly or silly than one or two.

No such effort is made.

Children are taught, with anguish and rebellion, to "take care of their clothes"—at least the effort is made to teach them. We seek also to make them "keep their clothes clean," a fruitless task, and injurious if accomplished. No healthy child can be a safe clothes-bearer. But no one teaches the child anything whatever about the nature and purpose of clothes—what they mean to humanity, and how to appreciate them.

The boy, becoming a youth, has his period of agitated interest in cut and buttons, in hats, socks, and ties; and presently, selecting in a limited range, decides on the kind of clothes he likes and wears them thereafter. Or else, using even less intellect, accepts what is given him by the tailor, or merely imitates his companions.

As said before, the higher state of development in men's clothing is due to their advanced social condition, to their economic status, and not to any special superiority of sex. A glance at the history of costume shows that men have eagerly worn all conceivable monstrosities, even to stuffing their trunks and doublets with bran, to the shaven head and powdered horsehair wig, to the shoe so long in its pipe-extended toe that it was fastened to the knee or even to the girdle. But men, as workers, have evolved farther in costume than have women.

The girl growing into youth and womanhood, finds nothing to check the doll-and-baby influences, or the imitative instinct. She finds, however, two new forces at work upon her—the pressing necessity of using dress as an avenue of sexuo-economic advantage, and the further demand for "style" as a means of social advancement.

Observe the cumulative forces by which she is influenced: (a) the primitive decorative taste of racial and personal childhood, carried on from doll to baby, and from baby to doll; (b) the imitative habit, so natural to the human race, and to its immediate progenitors, unchecked by the conscious application of the mind; (c) the tremendous compound force of the sex-motive with economic advantage; and (d) the desire for social advancement, as attained by clothes.

It is no wonder that women, so long as they were wholly uneducated and unused to any freedom, should have abjectly surrendered to such pressure as this. It is no wonder, either, that even today so many women able to balance results should deliberately choose the easiest way and gain their ends by dressing rather than by doing.

But it is grave cause for amazement that women of real ability, of clear strong minds, of high ethical sense, should allow this subject of clothing to remain without even intelligent consideration. The peculiar slavishness of their attitude would, one would think, rouse some smoldering feeling of rebellion. From sheer love of exercise, the subject, one would think, might attract the active mind, the efficient will.

No such desire is shown, no such effort made. "Fashion's Mandate" is accepted as if a revelation from heaven or a law of nature. In a current "Woman's Magazine" we are given a solemn "page" with the ukase from Paris. This is merely a letter from a correspondent, a person hired to tell the eager readers what they must do now, quickly, to obey this whirligig monarch.

"Most of the big coutouriers (an impressive word, meaning only dressmakers) here have decided to emphasize the figure in their new creations for the Fall and Winter."

"The figure claims their attention first, and the design, once so important, comes second."

"Hips are in evidence, and the slender waist has arrived."

"Paquin will favor wide skirts."

"Bernard, the leading Parisian tailor, says that straight skirts and kimono sleeves are at an end."

"Jenny will employ a profusion of narrow soutache on her lovely autumn dresses."

Well? These are statements which may be correct enough as to the intentions of Paquin, Bernard and Jenny—but what of it. What is this awed importance attached to the opinions and purposes of these tradespeople? If we see a page announcing that "Most of the big grocers have decided to emphasize cheese in their new stock"—do we therefore buy more cheese?

"Jones will favor old cheese."
"Brown, the leading wholesaler, says that Edam cheese and Neufchatel are at an end."
"Susie will employ a profusion of Limburger in her menus."

What of it? Does a conspiracy of tradesmen to force you to change your diet make a million women run headlong to discard the food they were eating and eat a new kind?

Only in dress, and almost wholly in the dress of women, is it possible to dictate to half the adult population as if they were a lot of hypnotized dummies.

"Fix your eyes on Me!" say the Leading Coutouriers. The eyes are fixed—glued—in silent adoration.
"Think exclusively about clothes in relation to the orders I give!"
They think, exclusively.
"Now then, attention! Act promptly please! Up with the waistline!"
It goes up.
"Down with the waistline!"
It goes down.
"Away with the waistline!"
It goes away.

The devotees are breathless with the speed of the changes and with their eager concentrated attention to see that their waistlines are correctly located.

"Trail your skirts in the mud!"
They trail them.
"Shorten your skirts halfway to the knee!" They shorten them.
"Tighten your skirts into a single trouser leg!" They tighten them.

Quite apart from the beauty, the truth, the comfort, the economy, the health involved in this matter of clothing, what is the matter with our women that they do not resent this insolent dictation?

By what Right does any man or group of men—and Jennys—issue orders to American women? By what Wrong, what weak compliance, what cowardice, what blank lack of thought, what creeping paralysis of the will do we take these orders and obey them? We search eagerly for them. We send "correspondents" to Paris to get them—in advance. We out-Herod Herod in fulfilling them, going quite beyond the intention of the Commander, so that our Rulers come over here and condemn us, to our faces, for our too-absolute submission.

Moreover, so sodden through and through are most women by this weird cult of style, that, wholly unaware of their own grotesque appearance, they criticize and ridicule other costumes which may be far more essentially beautiful than theirs. They measure one another by their clothes—not by their bodies, much less minds; and the standard of measurement is not the excellence of material used, the skill of its construction, its fitness to time, place, and occupation, its abstract beauty as a garment or its concrete beauty of becoming the wearer—none of these nor all of them weigh against the one question: "Do this woman's clothes obey orders?" If they do not, she is anathema.

One might expect this of women in the harem stage of development. We might understand it among those wretched traders in sex whose clothing is their signboard. We can appreciate it among those who spend their lives in trying to get invitations from their "social superiors," a game in which clothes are as much a signboard as in the other. But that comfortable matrons, working women, even many who think and teach, should also be blighted with this disastrous weakness, showing neither knowledge of aesthetics, economics, or hygiene in dress, but only the demand for Conformity—Obedience to Orders—is not only ludicrous but pathetic, not only pathetic, but dangerous.

Remember that this conformity is not to a fixed type, but is a frantic shadow-dance after constantly changing patterns. Remember that it occupies the minds of practically all women in so far as they are able to attain to it, and requires for fulfillment not only thought but constant labor. It is not only Flora McFlimsy but the loving mother in Barrie's exquisite picture, who worked so hard to remake her children's garments after the changes she glimpsed from the window.[2]

Remember that a constant active submission to orders—on any

line—is not only a temporary preventative of independent action, but tends to destroy the wish and the will for it.

Remember that the most important qualities of the human race are those which enable us to Think Freely and to Act Strongly on our own decisions.

Slowly and only recently we have struggled out of the age-old status of slavery, real chattel slavery. Slowly, recently, and only partially, have some nations broken loose from the Infallibility of the Church and the Divine Right of Kings. All the way through history we may see the Human Soul pushing, striving, toward freedom. Only with freedom comes progress, growth, the true unfolding of qualities and powers, the development of right relationships, which is our great Race Duty on the earth.

And here, in the very face of all our hard-won freedom, we see half the people contentedly, eagerly, delightedly, practicing this unspeakably foolish slavery to the whims and notions, and the economic demands, of a group of people less worthy to rule than any Church or Court of past—the daring leaders of the demi-monde, the poor puppets of a so-called "Society" whose major occupation is to exhibit clothes, and a group of greedy and presuming tradesmen and their employees.

These determine our fashions.

These give orders.

To these we, in our millions, submit.

Chapter Eleven

Fashion and Psychology

THERE is no least detail of human life which does not bear relation to the whole. There is no act, however trivial, which may not be called "right" or "wrong"—in relation to living.

In order to judge of the rightness and wrongness we must, of course, have some clear idea about living, about the Great Game, and our personal part in it.

When an individual's place and work in life call for some special costume it is easy to see what clothes are "right" and what "wrong." If in one's business it is necessary to change clothing often, or to change with speed, there is rightness and wrongness in those processes; but when we consider ordinary women's lives, the standard is not so clear.

What we have here to study is not the ethical quality of this or that costume, or of physical dexterity in donning or doffing it; but the ethics of Fashion, the psychology of Fashion, the relation of this habit of abject submissiveness to all the rest of life.

So unaccustomed are we to thinking about our clothing, to any real reasoning process as to its nature, quality and effect, that it seems absurd to attach a high psychological importance to this general subservience to Fashion.

Let us see:

We must first establish a common ground as to the nature and purpose of human life.

Without going into first causes or ultimate results, most of us will surely agree that our business on earth is to improve, personally and socially. We should grow better ourselves, and our children should be better than we are. We should improve the condition of living; improve in health, in beauty, in intelligence—all of us. We should improve our social and political relations, tending toward that Kingdom of Heaven on earth which religion commands, which evolution promises, and which human nature desires.

Very well. Then we may go on to say: Those acts are right which tend to bring about such improvement. Those ideas and emotions are right which tend to promote such acts. Those surroundings are right which tend to develop the ideas and emotions leading to such acts.

Very well again. Now suppose we show that a given act, such as docking the tails of Horses, tends to dull that sympathy with animals which not only attends high social progress but helps promote it; or that it tends to prevent the development of a sense of real beauty and thus again limits social progress; or that, if it be done by persons otherwise showing such sympathy or such beauty sense, then it necessarily maintains a break in the brain connection, a deep-seated inconsistency, which is a dangerous flaw in mental equipment, liable to do unexpected mischief at any point.

It may seem a simple and trivial thing, this mutilating an animal to save oneself trouble, or from a false and primitive beauty sense, yet its correlations and results are both complex and important.

So are all the connections between our various acts.

If one has a strong, consistent, normal brain, it cannot bear to be foolish in one place and wise in another; it must bring its acts into harmony. If on the contrary, one's brain is cheerfully unconscious of its inconsistencies, cannot even see them, perhaps; or, seeing, makes light of them, sees no harm in them—then that brain is not strong, consistent, normal.

In the huge tangle of unnecessary foolishness which keeps the world back from its natural health and happiness, two factors stand out before all; the one, that we do not seem able to see clearly and judge fairly as to our difficulties; the other that when we do see straight and judge truly we appear paralyzed in regard to action.

Take so simple a matter as the need of good roads in our country. This may be explained to a child of twelve, or less. A country with *no* roads is not civilized at all, is uninhabitable save by savages; a country with few and poor roads is thereby limited in its development. The better the roads, up to the full limit of its needs of transportation and travel, the better the country. Moreover, we do not plant a thick population and then make roads for them. No, we make roads and "develop the country"; the population comes and settles along the roads. We could promote the wealth of our country, improve its intelligence, health and happiness rapidly and steadily by a nation-wide improvement in roads. We have plenty of material for road-building. We know how. We have the requisite labor, labor demanding employment so loudly that we call it "a problem."

Well? Why do we not go to it—this problem—apply the labor to the materials and provide our country with the best roads in the world? There is no reason except, first, our inability to grasp large questions like this, however clear and simple; and second, our inability to act after we do understand.

There are thousands of such instances. And what has it to do with the dress of women?

This: Women are half the world. Because of their effect on the rest of it, as mothers and influencers of men, they are the more important half. A race of active and intelligent women, with men kept in harems, would make better progress than we see where the men keep the women in harems and try to be active and intelligent alone. Human progress in the hands of men is continually interfered with by their maleness, by the special weakness and irritability proper to their sex. They are peculiarly susceptible to drug habits, such as the common use of alcohol and nicotine; so lacking in self-control as to show a most deadly record of vice and crime with correlative diseases; and so inherently belligerent as to fill the world with fighting.

The natural qualities peculiar to women are those distinguishing motherhood; tendencies of love, of care and service, of creative industry, of all that develops the family group, and so leads on to higher forms. Even in their abnormal position of seclusion and dependence they have maintained in the home a good showing of many of the qualities we need to see in the world at large. Anything which tends to keep back our women, to prevent their physical, mental and moral growth, is a serious injury to the world.

We have previously discussed the influence of various articles of dress upon the minds and bodies of women; the present point is not the effect of any especial costume or piece of costume, but the effect of *following the fashions.*

Suppose that the fashions handed out to us were good ones; that the dresses and decorations were really beautiful, and in no way injurious. What we are to consider is not the effect of the fashion ordered, but the effect of obeying the orders.

Here we have our half the world, in the so-called civilized races, habitually submitting its mind to a brainless obedience.

A woman may have no knowledge of beauty, of anatomy, physiology, or hygiene; of textile art either in fabric or garment, or of decorative art in any form; and yet, if "the fashion" happens to be beautiful and suitable she is as wisely dressed as her wiser sisters. A woman may be past mistress of all that knowledge, and yet, if "the fashion" happens to be ugly and silly, she is as foolishly dressed as her foolish sisters. And both of them, in obeying orders, waive their own right of judgment, and, by disuse, lose the power.

The human brain, our transcendent racial advantage, is capable of steering and pushing us to the gates of heaven. Through its power of inhibition we are able to check primitive or disorderly impulses; through its power of volition we are able to behave better than we want to—so building the good habits of the future.

With no brains—no humanity. With little brains—little humanity. With weak, uncertain brains—weak and uncertain humanity. As the brain develops, widening in range of vision, perceiving closer relations, pushing to farther conclusions, and applying its ever-growing powers to conduct, so develops humanity.

We may become vastly learned in one line or another without this beneficent result. It is not the storage capacity of the brain that counts, nor even its reasoning power, if unused; it is knowledge, reasoning, *and* the effectual dominance of these qualities which make for true human progress.

So long as we "follow fashion" in clothing, by just so much are we incapacitated from ever improving our clothing.

The habit of submission absolutely prohibits the habit of judgment, of free choice and determined action.

Minor variations of a given style are offered, that we may think we are "choosing," but we may not choose outside that style. When women's hats were as big as fruit-baskets there were no small-crowned ones for sale—they were not made; the buyer had no choice but a choice of evils.

Moreover, the psychology of fashion is such that, after being surrounded with some abnormal hideous thing like those huge hats extinguishing a woman from eyebrow to shoulder, the beholder in course of time becomes accustomed to it, and a hat of normal shape and size looks dwarfed and abnormal.

Also the tradespeople, selling their "new styles," are wholly robbed of judgment by the swirling stream. They have no standard whatever, save that of fashion, and their ignorance coupled with their scorn, piles up the difficulties of the purchaser who would really like to choose wisely.

Dressmakers, when dresses are made to fasten in the back, profess to be unable to make them to fasten in front. Able or not, they refuse.

Apropos of that particular folly, cannot even a fashionable woman see the baby-like, doll-like, slave-like helplessness of her position! She is forced, absolutely compelled, to have her dress fasten in the back. *She* never thought of having it done that way. It is uncomfortable when done, difficult to do, and *utterly useless*. There is no shadow of reason for it. It may be done to little children or to idiots to prevent their taking their clothes off, but why a grown woman should be driven to ask help for that necessary act it is indeed hard to see. Very few women have maids. Most women made use of reluctant and justifiably scornful husbands. But what of those who had none?

I have heard a woman unblushingly state that, traveling alone, and stopping in a hotel, she sent for the bellboy to fasten her dress around her helpless form. What would women think of men who could not put on their own clothes? Fancy a man calling madly for someone to button his coat up the back for him!

Yet so blank are the minds of women of any sentiment or dignity, of independence, of anything whatever except fashionableness, in the matter of clothing, that they submitted to this ignominy for years—without protest.

Within my memory our "freeborn female citizens"—if women are citizens—have been the butt of humorists and satirists and the scorn of cynics for these excesses: (a) hoop-skirts; (b) the "Grecian bend"—a shameful misnomer—Greek indeed!—that kangaroo position; (c) the "tied back"—picture in Punch at the time shows fashionably dressed ladies who could not get in when they reached their ball—because it was upstairs! (d) the tight sleeve—they had to put their hats on first, the dress, or rather the "basque," afterward; (e) the "muttonleg sleeve"; (f) the trailing skirt—actually on the sidewalk, and with special "dust-ruffles" made to sew underneath to keep it from wearing out too fast!

Then, for a little while, appeared the one perfect dress which we have had in perhaps a century—a "Princess dress," comfortably fitted, wide enough to walk or run in, short enough for cleanliness and health, decent and beautiful in every respect.

Was this perfect dress due to any protest or demand from its wearers?

Not in the least. They did not even know it was perfect, but wore it with the same complacency they had shown in all the others, and gave it up as meekly at the next command.

The next (g) was the "sheath skirt," in which the woman cheerfully exhibited the full outlines of her gluteal muscles, and this soon became the "hobble skirt" (h), that contemptible stigma of imbecility, in which our women manacled their legs so contentedly.

Add to these conspicuous idiocies the enormous hats before mentioned; and never did women look more foolish than when they went about peering out from under their extinguishers like a butcher's boy with his basket over his head.

But they did not know they looked foolish. They had no acquaintance whatever with the true proportions of the human body, and the crowning dignity of the human head. They first made their heads into Ashantee mops by gigantic pompadours and then concealed them in these hats with the shape

> "Of an inverted wastebasket wherein
> The head finds lodgment most appropriate!"

What can account for this area of grovelling slavishness in minds otherwise independent? The explanation of the commanders is clear enough, but what is the explanation of the submitters?

It is this: When a given fashion is ordained, and the women look at it, they look with minds vacant of the bases of judgment and lacking the power of judgment. If you offer a musical performance to a person who has never heard any music, he has nothing to judge by but his own personal reaction. If you offer it to a person who has been obliged to hear every night of his life music of every description with no choice or study, he has only this personal reaction blurred into dullness by heterogenous experience. But if you offer that same performance to one skilled in music, either as a performer or a loving student, one who understands methods, and whose taste has been educated by hearing the best and by intelligent discussion—such a one can judge the performance more competently.

We shall never be competent to judge the merits of costume until we have full knowledge of its bases: of textile art as a great social power; of the history of dress, its evolution, its different periods, beauties, excesses, uglinesses, and gross follies. We should be grounded in the great distinctive styles of the world: the "straight cut" with what we glibly call the "kimono sleeve"; the crosswise cut, seen in the Medean robes of old, and only approximated now in the soft folds of a "circular" skirt or cloak; the "skirt" as a separate article—see Hottentots; the various leg coverings, and the adoption of trousers by men in the Occident, by women in the Orient—with reasons; and the other underlying divisions.

On historic charts a given article of clothing should be shown, expanding and contracting, developing in various lines, slowly in earlier times, faster now that the pressure of the tradesman has become more powerful. We should learn to recognize that Unknown Artist, the Composer in Cloth, that man or woman who loves to work in fabrics as sculptors love the clay, and who, if we knew enough to recognize them, would give us all manner of lovely and legitimate variations on a theme originally good.

With this we should be taught—children in schools—young folks in college—to recognize and ridicule the excesses of the past. Comparative exhibitions should be made of the wide range of "improvers" mankind has used; from the shameless "codpiece" men wore in Elizabethan days to the modest shoulder-pads of the present; the corset male and female—mostly female; the "bustles" and other kinds of stuffing with which women seek to supplement deficiencies; and, conversely, the "reducers" with which they seek to check redundancies.

Teach our children, clearly and strongly, to know foolishness in dress and to despise it.

Teach them to know the beauty and strength of the human body and to honor it.

Teach them to appreciate textile art as well as the others; to understand what is good material and to recognize it. And, with all the force of word and picture, with humor, satire, irony and scathing sarcasm, teach them to know and to despise all false and foolish dress.

Against the shameless pressure of those who make money by our idealessness, we should present a solid front of clear knowledge and trained judgment.

In this training there are several distinct lines of study, all of which need to be fully taught but all of which may be simplified so as to be easily learned. Only those who deeply loved the art and craft of cloth and costume making would study deeply, just as but few of us study music deeply, or architecture.

There is the line of physical beauty, involving health, vigor, freedom, grace, and the full and subtle range of personal expression. This last could be vividly and convincingly shown by careful use of models and made universally available by moving pictures. The lecturer on "Personal Expression in Dress" has on the platform models of distinct personal types. They are first shown all in similar dresses, and those of the simplest, most non-committal type, such, for instance, as a "union suit." While they are similarly clothed and standing in the same position, the speaker could point out the special power and dignity of bearing of A; the soft grace of B; the frail slenderness of C; the suggestion of alert activity of D; the dainty roundness of E.

The five next appear, still all alike, in a Turkish "ferigech," or a nun's costume, to show how all personal distinction may be lost, or at least blurred, by some forms of dress.

Then some well known types of costume should be used on all five, as the Japanese, the Chinese, the Greek, the Quaker. This would show how a good type of dress, though more "becoming" to some than to others, does justice to all, and allows of much personal expression.

As much of this could be shown as there was time for, and while wearing these typical costumes the models should take various positions and perform various actions, as to stand, sit, stoop, walk, run, dance, and so on, showing that a given dress is more suitable for some attitudes and actions than for others.

Then, taking one model at a time, she should appear in various dresses, chosen to obscure, exaggerate, or to properly bring out her special characteristics, closing with the whole five shown at their worst—and at their best.

This part should involve a special study of becomingness, and be carried out in detail. For instance, the five should be shown in profile, the hair smoothly drawn back and around to the side of the head away from the audience, merely to show as far as possible with the hair on just what kind of heads they had, and how they held them.

Then the same simple coiffure should be shown upon all of them. Then, treating one at a time, the hair should be arranged in various ways, with careful pointing out by the lecturer of what was done to the face and head by each arrangement. The medieval Italian idea of feminine beauty, with an extremely high forehead, should be sharply contrasted with the sensuous unintelligent effect of hair worn low to the eyebrows.

Then each coiffure should be arranged to the best personal effect. Incidentally it should be shown how a given style of hair dressing is related to a given costume, exhibiting, for instance, that lately seen blunder of hair massed on the back of the neck accompanied by a Medician collar.

Again a given model should be shown in a plain and beautiful dress, coiffure, and hat, and the principles of decoration illustrated. On her head with its smoothly coiled, richly braided or soft piled hair should be placed a variety of ornaments, first separately, and then together, showing the effect of right, wrong, and excessive ornament. A hat, perfect in outline, and quite becoming, should be made imperfect and unbecoming by ill-placed or excessive decoration, and restored to beauty by true decoration. Simple illustrations here are the "glen-garry," or the Tyrolese hat, with a simple, alert little feather, and the cavalier hat, with its sweeping plume. Reverse these ornaments and observe the effect.

So with the dress. A softly gleaming silk hanging in rich folds should be murdered before the eyes of the spectators by heavy rigid bands of trimming; a neat and satisfying tailored suit made ridiculous by lace and beads; a filmy muslin weighted to extinction by spangles and fringe.

In the end each model should appear, in a perfect type of the kind of dress best suited to her own characteristics, and in itself a beautiful costume, in no way interfering with full freedom of action.

Lectures like that would be immensely instructive, and also vividly interesting. We need a large and growing body of information, a clear, strong presentation, given far and wide, to all our people, men and women alike—for men are very largely responsible for the folly of women's dresses, first by designing and second by admiring them.

No, Mr. Smith, this does not mean that you personally admire the dress your wife has on, but it does mean that you and your brethren admire and pay court to the "stylishly dressed" women—and your wife knows it.

Besides this trained knowledge of the physical side of dress we must establish a deep sense of its ethical values. Here again we reach our psychology, the mental reactions both of individual costumes, and of this underlying weakness which allows us to take the costumes given us with neither choice nor protest.

The condition of the world today surely shows that there are deep wrongs in the body politic. One after another may be pointed out, all serious, all undeniable. But among them all this functional disturbance in our mental action is not only serious in itself, but works incalculable evil in its results. We do not meet the problems of life with clear, unbiased minds, free minds, strong minds, minds able to decide wisely and to act upon decision.

Dress is not the only subject of decision in life, and women are not the only people, but they are a very weighty half, and dress is to them a matter of pressing importance. If women once lifted their heads in nation-wide revolt on this one field of action; if they determined once and for all: "We will no longer be the walking mannequins for these cloth peddlers"; if they would begin and continue the exercise of their minds on this question—they would find it easier to exercise them on others. No matter how wise and strong a person may be on some lines, if they are weak and foolish on others it weakens the whole character. Conversely, no matter how weak and foolish one is, to begin to be wise and strong on any line helps in all. The brainless submissiveness of women in the matter of fashion helps to maintain the brainless submissiveness of men in the matter of their fashions, the sway of custom, of habit, the general weakness of acting without first deciding and then acting on decision.

The world is full of ancient habits, customs, methods of doing things, attitudes of mind. The whole progress of the world is in steadily outgrowing its ancient limitations. More than anything else we need the power to See; to look out over the confusion of our environment, to recognize the general direction in which we should all move, and our own part in it; and then, most important of all, we need Power To Act.

It is an interesting fact in psychology that power gained in one direction is useful in all. "He that is faithful over a few things, I will make him ruler over many."[1] Courage, patience, perseverance—whatever virtues we practice at home or in school or among our friends—those virtues are ours to use in important public measures. If our women freed themselves once and for all from this utterly unnecessary slavery, began to use their own judgment and their own will on their clothes, the psychic effect would be of immeasurable importance, not only to themselves, but to their sons, brothers, and husbands.

The destruction of a bloated artificial market would be a good thing economically, a very good thing; the increased health and beauty of our womankind would be another good thing; but best of all would be the lifted head, the daring eye, the clear judgment, the strong, efficient will. A race of women free and strong, healthy, active, graceful, swift; a race of women who know what they want and why, and who act firmly to get it—these will give us a race of men similarly strengthened.

Chapter Twelve

Hope and Comfort

IN LATER years, when the human mind is free and active, it will seem strange indeed that any appeal was needed to induce people to make such an easy change for the better as a change in dress.

Some steps in social progress are long, slow and difficult, such as the breaking down of race-hatreds and class prejudices; others are quite beyond the reach of this generation and only to be worked toward, without looking for immediate accomplishment, such as the complete rearrangement of the economic position of women. The comfort we may feel in facing this question of dress for women, is that, in one sense, their very weakness is their strength. They have no prejudice whatever against any kind of fabric, color, or shape. They are too thoroughly "broken" by long submission to enforced changes to have any opposing force against another change. So we have no definite antagonism to overcome, only the will-less waste of unused minds to enter and develop.

Moreover, there is another comfort, a large one. The adoption of wiser and more beautiful clothes hurts no one but the tradesmen who now profit by our foolishness; and only hurts them in two ways; in the matter of limiting their excessive production, which will, of course, be cut down when we apply intelligence to costume, and in the special work of designing an unnecessary flood of "novelties" to allure constant purchasing. We must allow fairly for this degree of opposition, and it is not inconsiderable. The whole "dry goods" trade would be curtailed, and the dressmakers, milliners, customers of all sorts, and makers of innumerable flimsy patterns—all these would strongly object to a reduction in their trade.

But just as each new mechanical advance limits, changes, or puts an end to, certain employments, so will such an advance as this. Men did not continue to wear those awful horsehair wigs because of any sympathy with the barbers and wig-makers thrown out of work when wigs went out of fashion. A certain number of workers will always be required to make the cloth and the garments we need, and a certain number of designers also to fill the world with beauty, real beauty, of new materials and new patterns in fabric, dress and ornament. But there is no justice nor economy in expecting us to wear foolish, ugly and superfluous things just because a lot of people want to be paid for making them.

We should remember, also, that as against the protest of these tradesmen and craftsmen at any interference with their bloated enterprises, we must set the present protest of great numbers of work people who are continually injured by the rapid fluctuations in fashion. There are the "seasonal" trades where great numbers are employed at certain times of year, and thrown out of work at others; and there are other great numbers always learning to make some new article in sudden demand and then discharged when it is as suddenly not wanted.

One of the many valuable results of a healthy market for dress materials and clothing manufacture would be the steady work for a regular number of people. Then a far higher degree of skill could be developed, a deeper understanding and love for the work. With this, supporting it and growing by it, would appear the strong good taste, the definite trained beauty sense which can never find a foothold in our perpetual cyclone of new fashions. Most of us are whirled along with it, deafened and stunned by the speed of the current; some cower in storm-cellars, as it were, in the peaceful monotony of some prescribed costume or the dull submission of utter poverty. With real intelligence in active use we should find our equilibrium, to the advantage of the producer as well as the consumer. The producers ought not to object, but they will.

As against the protest of this group of workers, we shall have the supports of artists and sculptors, of physicians and hygienists, of all reasonable and far-seeing people, men or women. We shall have, too, the satisfaction of increased incomes, increased by not spending inordinate amounts for unnecessary things. We shall have clean consciences, artistic and economic; healthier and more beautiful bodies, stronger and cleaner minds—all this is our comfort and our hope.

Just what is it that we hope for? Many have asked me: "What do you want us to wear? What costume do you propose?"

Here is seen an instant proof, if more proof were needed, of the effect of long submission. We do not find an eager desire to be free, and to be able, at last, to follow one's own taste and preference. There is no demand at all from personal choice, only the meek turning from one master to another: "What do *you* say we should wear?"

One hears women, feebly remonstrating against "the tyranny of fashion," wish that someone would design "a perfect costume." There is no perfect costume for everyone to wear all the time. Even an individual, unless spending an entire life in doing one kind of work, would not find any costume permanently perfect. No, the hope of the world in this matter of clothing is not in some revelation of A Perfect Dress; it is in the development of a personal taste, an educated taste; and, with it, a strong effective will. Clothes must differ as people differ, else they fail of one great function, that of personal expression. They must differ, of course, with occupation, as, in many cases they do now. No one need fear a new regime in which one costume is imposed on all women. This would not be new at all; it is found now in the Orient.

One new regime offers to us a condition like this:

First. So high a standard of physical health, activity and beauty, that we shall not consent to wear anything injurious to the body, or in any way limiting its powers.

Second. So keen a sense of true economy, that we shall not be willing to buy poor garments, or to throw away good ones. We shall become so proud of our own skill in selection or construction that we shall boast: "I have worn this six years!" instead of our present silly pride in "the very latest."

Third. Such an educated taste in the field of textile art, and in the history of design and the evolution of dress, that we shall admire and appreciate a piece of goods or a garment as real connoisseurs, not, as now, measuring only by dates—"How new is it?"

Fourth. So true a feeling for personal expression that a woman's clothes will be part of herself, governed first by her physique and occupation, and then subtly modified by her moods.

Some women would like many changes of costume; they should

have them. Some would be grateful beyond words for a single suitable and comfortable gown which could be put on and fastened with one button; they should have it. Some would show ingenuity in devising changes; others would gladly accept designs by those more clever.

The results would be these:

The elimination of all injurious articles of clothing, like high heels and corsets, and of all unnecessary and false articles of clothing, such as pads and bustles; also the reduction in volume of the trade in clothing to normal dimensions, thus assuring an immense saving of money, of time, of human labor.

A great increase in physical health and beauty, affecting not only the women but the whole race.

A beautiful development of the real textile art, and of the allied arts of design and construction of clothing.

A new world of loveliness and honor in dress, replacing the present one, in which the costumes of women are so often things to laugh at, to condemn, and to despise.

There is much confusion of idea on the subject of beauty and sex attraction, many fearing that if women's clothes were not constructed with a definite sex-appeal, they would not be beautiful.

This is an error. Human beauty is something far beyond sex beauty. Many a woman may fall far short of even our standards of true beauty, and yet be irresistible to the opposite sex. Others are nobly beautiful and yet fail to charm.

The beauty we need is human beauty; that grave, sweet, noble womanhood which is conscious of its high place and power; the beauty of dignity and freedom, not the hectic flutter of spangles designed to attract the eye of the necessary male.

It is clear that one of the strongest forces helping on such a change in the dress of women is that basic power of freedom. The penniless dependent woman may not dress as she likes, but must dress as she has to. Free women will demand freedom in choice of their own clothes.

Another helpful force is the increasing differentiation of women as they take up new occupations and specialize in them. While women all follow one trade, the unpaid labor in the home, it is far easier to dress them according to arbitrary fashions than it will be when they become more strongly individualized.

Political independence is also a great help. It adds to the sense of power, the feeling of personal dignity. The slave in the harem or the cook in the kitchen may be willing to dress like a doll or a tame monkey, but Queen Demos will hold a new attitude toward life.

Such change for the better in the clothing of women will greatly affect the feeling of men toward them, and, in itself, help to promote their progress. The little boy would not so soon look down on the little girl if she and he were dressed alike. He despises, and with reason, that silly, bobbing, enormous bow of bright ribbon on the head which answers no purpose whatever except to scream: "This is a girl." He despises, and with reason, the frail material and foolish shape of her frocks, which last either prevents free action, or accompanies it with unseemly exposure.

The girl child is by nature as big and strong, as enterprising and agile, as the boy. It is by artificial means that we divide them and restrict her, at the same time fostering in her, with elaborate care, the sex-consciousness and "clothes-consciousness" which hamper all her later life.

The young man would find it easier to maintain a hearty comradeship with young women, if the young women were not dressed to attract. There is no better safeguard for the excitable emotions of youth than free friendly association on equal terms, thus maintaining mutual acquaintance and respect on the ground of a common humanity, instead of adding an artificial mystery and distinction to the natural attraction of the sexes.

The heaviest charge of all the many that may be brought against the dress of women is its being so predominantly sexual. We should take a lesson from the "lower animals," remembering that their special sex-adornments are not only confined to the male, but often appear only in the mating season. We have not only put the tail of the peacock on the back of the pea-hen, but the poor thing must needs strut and spread it all the time; she must, too, if he feeds her for her beauty. He spreads that blue-green splendor for mating purposes, and sheer male pride; she would have to spread it whenever she was hungry.

The whole field of morbid sex-activity, which so evilly distinguishes our race, would be most healthfully affected by a desexualizing of women's clothes.

The child's natural love of beauty should be carefully developed, gratified and trained, in boy and girl alike. The young people should be encouraged to study beauty, and provided with really beautiful garments—both boys and girls.

A return to normal in the dress of women would be accompanied by a similar normality in the dress of men. It is no advantage to the world to have men as sad-colored and monotonous as they are now.

To put it briefly, we should so change our costumes as to lower sex-distinction and heighten race-distinction.

The freeing of individual taste in women would be promptly reflected in men; and the higher beauty sense now shown by women would be inherited and trained in sons as well as daughters.

It may be well to offer to our anemic imaginations, pale and prostrate from long disuse, one or two concrete suggestions: things possible to buy and wear now.

Knit underwear in a wide variety, or its equivalent in muslin or silk, may be obtained in simple and comfortable shapes; one-piece affairs of skirt and bodice together, or drawers and bodice together. Knickerbockers also are available. Also certain forms of "brassiere" which answer the purpose of a bust supporter, when needed. Long stockings may be gartered with no injury to the body by a loose hip-girdle, coming below the abdominal curve and held securely by the heavier muscles at side and rear.

Shoes that are neither ugly nor injurious may be wrung from reluctant tradesmen; some few manufacturers make a specialty of such. A continued demand would of course increase the supply.

Hats, just at present, may be found in thoroughly good shapes and sizes.

In all this there is no great difficulty save in the matter of shoes; yet even there the French heel, and almost as high Cuban heel, may be kicked out of existence in a year's time by the simple process of not buying them. The steady demand of thousands of women for low heels would bring them as fast as the factories could turn them out.

As to dresses, it is also possible at the present time, December, 1915, to buy ready-made, or have constructed by temporarily complacent makers, an extremely comfortable and pretty kind of dress. There are also many kinds which are neither, but the pleasant thing is that any good ones are available.

The new fashion of high fur collars, now patiently being accepted by the same women who have been baring their bronchial region to all the winds that blew, need not be accepted; nor the unnecessarily voluminous skirt.

These things are merely mentioned to show that there is an "isle of safety" just now for those who wish to begin to be sensible.

The second step is to stick to it—to refuse to give up the sensible for the silly.

The third, and most important, is to strike out for oneself; to cultivate an original distinctive personal taste; to invent for oneself, or to choose a special personal style and hold to it.

The fourth is to initiate a new industry, a new kind of dressmaker's establishment.

Let us enter one, one that is all that it should be, a "palace of industry" indeed.

In the reception rooms are casts of noble statues, pictures of typical historic dresses, books on the evolution of costume and on textile and decorative art. Also most interesting cabinets, containing little figurines, with dresses of certain periods, races, or arranged to indicate the lines of growth and decadence in a given fashion; as for instance the increase in the number of starched petticoats which immediately preceded the crinoline—I knew a lady who wore nine, going to a party about 1850—and then the narrower bell-shaped ones in which the crinoline dwindles to extinction in the early seventies.

There should be great sample books of various fabrics, patterns of laces and the like; a full and reliable choosing ground.

Then comes the larger exhibition room, with samples of all standard fabrics, and where many types of costume are shown on dummies, on models seen in action, on the purchaser who wishes to try the effect. Huge mirrors should be here, and deep closets full of lovely sample robes.

The consulting expert would be a person of wide experience and thorough education, with a keen color sense, and a sensitive perception of personal distinction—a sort of diagnostician and prescriber—to point out one's special type and kind of garment indicated. Here one could express and defend one's preferences, call for certain colors and combinations, and be intelligently and sympathetically met. A rather blundering description of what one had in mind would be helped out by quick reference to book, picture, or figurine, and a desired effect immediately illustrated on the living model.

"That's it!" cries the purchaser, delighted. "I knew it would be pretty. Make me one like that!"

If one had no choice, even among the offered samples, one might safely submit oneself to this expert. Shape, size, coloring, action, all carefully studied; such and such kinds of dress would be suggested; and people who do not like to bother about their clothes could "put themselves in the hands" of such a competent and disinterested guide as contentedly as they now commit themselves to the tender mercies of the fashion-makers.

The designing room would be like an architect's office—wide-windowed, clean, with great drawing tables and all the materials for line and color treatment; and the workroom, light, airy and beautiful, be filled with efficient needlewomen who had all been fully educated in their profession and loved it.

Now think again of a new kind of wardrobe at home. Think of the deep satisfying peace of having worked out the kind of costume which absolutely suited you, from the innermost to the outermost garment. Then to be able, without fuss or worry, to have made up, or to buy ready-made, a sufficient number of those perfectly satisfying garments; and then not to have to think of clothes again till they began to wear out!

The result is not monotony; nothing like the monotony of the present, where each and all must wear what "they" are wearing, whether they look well in it or not.

Some women would perhaps choose to wear always one kind of dress, but not many. Almost all of us like a change now and then. And there might be a thousand changes, yet, always beauty.

If some plump little curly-head preferred a Dolly Varden kind of dress of brightest figured chintz, she might wear it uncriticized by the side of another who insisted on a straight, long-sleeved, medieval gown of heavy silk; or still another who chose the slender "Empire" style in sheer muslin, and was beautified therein.

The differences we now find in the ever-revolving wheel of changing fashions we might still have, all at once and all the time—if we wanted them. Now we are all alike in one kind of foolish dress, until we are all alike in another. Then we could all be different, as different as in a fancy dress ball, if we so preferred.

The probability, however, is something like this: In the interests of comfort and convenience in ordinary work, women will become largely similar in dress through business hours; not as drearily identical as men are now, but still similar. Where the occupation agrees, the costume should agree, within reason. But when working hours are over, at home, or at play, anywhere, the whole world of women could blossom out to their heart's content, in beauty as varied as the flowers.

The human body is all one living thing. We cannot have disease in one part, and all the rest remain perfectly healthy. Even neglect of a given part, with its progressive atrophy, injures the circulation and general health. So with the human mind. The most elaborate education of one part does not make an intelligent person, if the rest remains a blank. Even the exercise of the reasoning faculty, on some subjects, does not make a reasonable being if the brain is never used on others.

So long as we remain positively foolish or negatively unreasoning, in any large department of life, the harmonious development of the mind is checked. This matter of the dress of women is mainly important as it affects the minds of women, and so the mind of the whole world. It is of measureless importance to our progress that women rapidly advance in all human powers and faculties. That advance is feared, disliked, and opposed on the ground that women are creatures of sex, whose place in life is wholly functional, limited to the fulfillment of sex relations, and of a group of low-grade, aborted industries practiced in the home.

The progress of women has been so far attained by colossal efforts, through which it has been proved, over and over, that women have human faculties as well as feminine ones. It is on the visible achievements of women that the change in public opinion turns. In our present stage of progress one of the strongest deterrent factors is the archaic absurdity of women's clothes.

They are now eagerly asking, demanding the ballot. The earnest speaker says: "The use of the ballot is human. I am a human being; treat me as such." But what the man sees, in the shop windows which leave no inmost secret of under-clothing concealed, and on the bare-necked, bare-shouldered, bare-backed, bare-chested and bare-axillaed ladies at dinner and at dance, is a species of dress which fairly screams at him: "I am a Female! Treat me as such!"

And he does.

It is inconceivable to the masculine mind that a being capable of wearing those ultra-sexual shoes—shoes the entire purpose of which is to make of the foot an alluring ornament; or those under-garments so unmistakably created to be looked through, not in the least to clothe and cover, but to stimulate the imagination, to be more exciting than a decent nudity; or those evening gowns (unworthy of that decent name) which are mere casual draperies, appearing in immediate danger of coming off, and meant to appear that way—dresses so worse than sleeveless as to require the use of a razor under the arm, in order that there may not be exhibited what even our present shamelessness is a little ashamed to show—it is inconceivable to him that such a being is a reasonable being, a human being, anything but a Female with the largest of *F's*.

Can we blame the masculine mind?

Can we with any logic demand one kind of freedom, while visibly willing to submit to the senseless dominion of fashion?

Of course, if the masculine mind were wholly reasonable itself it would see that the pot cannot call the kettle black and expect the kettle to make no retort. Women may well point to the eighty-five million dollar tobacco crop shown in the report of 1911, or to the two-billion, two-hundred and thirty-three million, four-hundred and twenty thousand, four hundred and sixty-one gallons of spirits, malt liquors and wines consumed in these United States in one year, 1913.[1] So long as the weak foolishness of men gives way to drug habits like these, it ill becomes them to say that the foolishness of women unfits them for the ballot. If unwisdom, or even wickedness were the measure of unfitness to vote, we should have a most restricted election.

But recrimination defends neither party. Men, with all their sins upon their heads (and also upon the heads of their wives and children) are still able to keep the world moving, while women are now claiming the right and the duty of helping in the process, and even asserting that they can move it to better ends.

It is the woman who must ask of the man the further opportunity to prove her wisdom, her high purposes, her effective human power. Such being her position today, it is immeasurably important that she should stand above all reproach. She has shown a cleaner record in vice and crime; she is proven industrious and faithful; she is, for the most part, a wise and careful spender of her husband's earnings; she still holds, in spite of all her limitations, a high place in man's esteem.

What then will be her place when she outgrows those limitations? When men see about them strong, sensible, active fellow-citizens, able and vigorous in body and mind, instead of these highly decorative objects, toddling about on their silly little heels, having to be helped on or off a street car, always inviting the open stare or furtive glance of superficial admiration.

The coming change in the Dress of Women is not so much a change of costume as a change of mind. Also it is a change of body. It is as if the women ceased to be dwarfs and suddenly grew up, grew to full human stature. It means a different kind of women; women with a new kind of pride, a new dignity, a new honor; women who with a few years of freedom and well-used judgment will marvel at the strange hypnotism which for so long has made them willingly ridiculous.

This is not a movement for dress reform. It does not require either a special kind of costume, or any laborious banding together to support one another in timid advancement, as, in the period of street-sweeping skirts there was a little society of women who wore short skirts on rainy days—"The Rainy Daisies," they were called.

All that is needed is the use of the individual judgment, the individual will, and both grow stronger with that use. There are no real lions in the path—nothing but mere false ideas. We slavishly do as we are told under the impression that something terrible will happen to us if we do not. But nothing does happen. How could it? There are no legal penalties for being sensible.

You say: "Oh, but I could not do it alone! If I wore low heels I should be conspicuous!"

Remember that you are not alone; there are millions of others, all in the same frame of mind; all waiting in their chronic submissiveness for somebody else to move first. Yet women have not lacked strength or courage to meet real danger. They stood with their men to fight the savages in pioneer days. They went to the stake as bravely as did men. They need only to see the importance, the duty, of this change, and they will make it easily. Here is no stake, no lion, no savage, nothing to fear but the adverse comment of people you know to be foolish—whereas at present women boldly sustain adverse comment from the wisest.

Shall women, who in their folly have not been moved by the jeering ridicule of the wisdom of all the ages, flinch now, when their growing wisdom shall meet the ridicule of a dwindling group of fools? They who have been conspicuous by their folly for so long, ought not to shrink from becoming conspicuous by their wisdom.

Man's contempt for the excesses of women's dress has its root in a deep-seated instinct, an instinct which knew she is not the one designed by nature to strut and flaunt in gorgeous plumage.

The majesty of womanhood will shine out in a far nobler splendor when she drops forever her false decoration, and learns that beauty lies in truth, in dignity, in full expression of our highest human powers.

Notes

CHAPTER ONE

1. "Gunga Din" was published in 1840 and collected in the *Barrack-Room Ballads* of British author Rudyard Kipling (1865–1936).

2. Thorstein Veblen (1857–1929) was an American economist and social scientist. Reference is to Veblen's first book, *The Theory of the Leisure Class: An Economic Study in the Evolution of Institutions* (New York: Macmillan, 1899).

CHAPTER TWO

1. Thomas Carlyle (1795–1881) was a leading Scottish historian and essayist during the Victorian era. His *Sartor Resartus* (1836) was then a popular mix of autobiography and philosophical rumination.

2. Charles Reade (1814–1884) was an English writer of serious social novels and dozens of melodramatic plays. Reference is to Reade's *Propria quae maribus: A jeu d'esprit; and The Box Tunnel: A Fact* (Boston: Ticknor and Fields, 1857).

3. For a contemporary sampling of the discussion concerning the international dress reform movement, see: Charlotte Perkins Gilman, "Why These Clothes?," *The Independent* (March 2, 1905: 466–469); Charlotte Perkins Gilman, "Symbolism in Dress," *The Independent*, Vol. 58 (June 8, 1905:

1294–1297); E. Oppler-Legbaud, "The German Dress Reform Movement," *The Independent*, Vol. 59 (August 31, 1905: 489–493); "The German and American Dress Reform," *The Independent*, Vol. 59 (August 31, 1905: 524–526); M. Cauer, "Dress Reform in Germany," *The Independent*, Vol. 63 (October 24, 1907: 993–997); "Dress and Its Relation to Life," *The Craftsman*, Vol. 11 (November, 1906: 269–271); William I. Thomas, "The Psychology of Woman's Dress," *The American Magazine* Vol. 67 (November, 1908: 66–72); M. G. Sutton, "Women and Dress," *Harper's Bazaar*, Vol. 44 (May 1910: 327); S. Bernhardt, "Can the American Woman Design Her Own Clothes?," *Ladies Home Journal*, Vol. 29 (April, 1912: 29); Ida M. Tarbell, "Extravagance in Dress," *Ladies Home Journal*, Vol. 30 (May, 1913: 26); N. W. Putnam, "Fashion and Feminism," *The Forum*, Vol. 52 (October, 1914: 580–584).

4. Gilman alludes here to the American writer Nathaniel Hawthorne's (1850) *The Scarlet Letter*, in which Hester Prynne is forced to wear a scarlet letter "A" on her dress to punish her for having committed adultery.

CHAPTER THREE

1. "September Morn" was painted by Paul Emile Joseph Chabas (1869–1937). Chabas was a French artist whose first painting on this theme, "Joyful Pastime," depicted a group of women playing at water's edge, a work that received the Prix de Salon in 1899.

2. Gilman's construct, "individual-social existence," astutely anticipates Anthony Giddens' concept of "the double hermeneutic," an insightful term promulgated in Giddens' *Sociology: A Brief but Critical Introduction* (San Diego: Harcourt Brace Jovanovich, 1987).

3. Gilman's expository constructions here suggest only that she intends the Australian Aborigines and the South Sea Islanders of her era as examples of her assertions. The complexity of non-modern social groups was often underestimated by Western social scientists such as Gilman, but her points remain essentially valid: indeed, the native people of Australia have survived into the twenty-first century and the South Sea Islanders did once enjoy a lively society free from the intrusions of complex scientific, technological, and bureaucratic structures.

CHAPTER FOUR

1. Mrs. Alexander Walker, *Female Beauty, As Preserved and Improved by Regimen, Cleanliness and Dress, and Especially by the Adaptation, Colour and Arrangement of Dress, as Variously Influencing the Forms, Complexion, and Expression of Each Individual, and Rendering Cosmetic Imposition Unnecessary*, revised by Sir Anthony Carlisle (New York: Scofield and Voorhies, 1840).

2. Lola Montez, *The Arts of Beauty* (New York: Dick and Fitzgerald, 1858). Montez noted: "The following classical synopsis of female beauty, which has been attributed to Felibien, is the best I remember to have seen." Montez's reference is, presumably, to André Félibien (1619–1695), a Frenchman who wrote widely on the arts, architecture, and art history.

3. While Gilman added the imperative phrase "should be" to Montez's sentence paraphrasing Félibien, the imperative here is fully consistent with Montez's intent. Compare Gilman's text with the reprint of Montez's *The Arts and Secrets of Beauty* (New York: Chelsea House, 1969: 2–3).

4. Gilman's reference to "the great statue from Melos" is, presumably, to the ancient statue of Aphrodite, better known as the Venus de Milo, and now at the Louvre, in Paris. The statue was found on the Island of Melos in 1820 and is believed to have been carved about 150 BC.

5. Divigation is, apparently, a Gilmanism meaning divergence and variety.

CHAPTER FIVE

1. Rudyard Kipling, *The Vampire* (London: The New Gallery, 1897), and subsequently issued in the United States in *Departmental Ditties, The Vampire, Etc.* (New York: Brentano's, 1899). The first stanza reads:

> A fool there was and he made his prayer
> (Even as you and I!)
> To a rag and a bone and a hank of hair
> (We called her the woman who did not care)
> But the fool he called her his lady fair—
> (Even as you and I!)

2. For a more recent theoretical exposition on "fun," "good times," and related sociological concepts, see Mary Jo Deegan, *American Ritual Dramas: Social Rules and Cultural Meanings* (Westport, CT: Greenwood Press, 1989); and *The American Ritual Tapestry* (Westport, CT: Greenwood Press, 1998).

3. Cleopatra VII Thea Philopator (69BC–30BC) was an Egyptian queen, a lover of Julius Caesar, and subsequently the wife of Mark Anthony; Ninon de Lenclos (1620–1705) was a noted French courtesan who espoused an Epicurean philosophy and wrote *La Coquette vengée* ("The Coquette Avenged") in 1659; Jeanne Françoise Julie Adélaide Bernard Récamier (1777–1849) was a wealthy hostess whose salon attracted noted members of French society, including Mme de Staël and François Chateaubriand.

4. The source of this ballad is unknown to the editors. F. M. Tuttle, an authority on such matters, observed recently that the lyrics share several interesting affinities with ballads from Appalachia (personal communication).

CHAPTER SIX

1. Dolly Varden (ca. 1871–1955) was, at the turn of the last century, a well-known American circus aerialist and equestrienne.

2. "Beauty unadorned is adorned the most," is a line in Charles Waddell Chestnutt's novel, *The House Behind the Cedars* (Boston: Houghton, Mifflin, 1900: 135). Chestnutt (1858–1932) was an early African-American progressive novelist known for short stories based on folklore. He was awarded the Spingarn Medal in 1928.

CHAPTER SEVEN

1. Joseph Marie Jacquard (1752–1834) devised and exhibited in 1801 an improved loom for weaving complex patterns.
2. Sir Ernest Henry Shackleton (1874–1922) was an explorer who led the British Antarctic Expedition during 1907–1909. Shackleton ventured again to Antarctica in 1914, returning to England in 1916.
3. Pergola, a balcony or arbor.
4. Maurice Polydore-Marie-Bernard Mæterlinck (1862–1949) was a Belgian symbolist writer who received the Nobel Prize for literature in 1911; O. Henry (the pseudonym of William Sydney Porter, 1862–1910) was a popular American writer of short fiction that celebrates the lives of ordinary people; Robert William Chambers (1865–1933) was a prolific American author of popular novels and short stories.
5. Thorstein Veblen, *Theory of the Leisure Class*, op cit.
6. Settlement work refers to service in one of hundreds of American social settlements, such as Chicago's Hull-House (where Gilman was a resident in 1895 and a frequent visitor until 1899) and Unity Settlement (where Gilman also served briefly as a resident). The ethos and dynamics of the many settlements in the United States varied widely, ranging from strict religious persuasions, through charitable, ameliorative and even socialist activities, to social scientific research. For a general survey, see Robert A. Woods and Albert J. Kennedy, *Handbook of Settlements* (New York: Charities Publications Committee, Russell Sage Foundation, 1911); for the sociological aspects of Hull-House, see Mary Jo Deegan, *Jane Addams and the Men of the Chicago School, 1892–1918* (New Brunswick, NJ: Transaction Books, 1988); and for Gilman's Chicago settlement work at Hull-House and Unity, see Mary Jo Deegan, "Gilman's Sociological Journey from *Herland* to *Ourland*," in Gilman's *With Her in Ourland: Sequel to Herland*, edited by Mary Jo Deegan and Michael R. Hill (Westport, CT: Greenwood Press, 1997: 17–26).

CHAPTER EIGHT

1. By, "gigantic caterpillars," Gilman refers, presumably, to feather boas.
2. The first "Audubon Society" was formed in 1886 to honor John James Audubon (1785–1851), the American naturalist. The National Association of Audubon Societies was organized in 1905. The association supported pas-

sage of the New York Audubon Act in 1911 that prohibited selling feathers of wild birds native to New York.

3. The theoretical concept of use value—and its contrast with the exchange value of a commodity—is integral to Karl Marx's (1818–1883) economic analysis of society in *Capital.*

4. Valenciennes is a costly lace made in the French city of the same name and also in Belgium.

CHAPTER NINE

1. George Fox (1624–1691) was an English clergyman who founded the Society of Friends, more popularly known as Quakers.

2. Sir James Matthew Barrie (1860–1937) was a Scottish novelist and playwright, best known for his play *Peter Pan, The Boy Who Wouldn't Grow Up. The Little Minister* (New York: Street and Smith, 1891), is one of Barrie's sentimental novels.

3. Gilman's use here of a base-to-superstructure construction parallels the logic earlier employed in Marx's single-minded theoretical analysis of capital.

4. Gilman's resort to a bad/good dichotomy remains surprisingly useful today. For more recent refinement, see G. L. Fox, " 'Nice Girl': Social Control of Women Through a Value Construct," *Signs*, Vol. 2, No. 4, 1977: 805–817; and, for a worked application, see Michael R. Hill and Mary Jo Deegan, "The Female Tourist in a Male Landscape," *CELA Forum* (Council of Educators in Landscape Architecture), Vol. 1, No. 2, 1982: 25–29.

5. George Sand's *Consuelo* was published in French in 1842 and subsequently translated into English by Francis G. Shaw. Sand was the pseudonym of Aurore-Lucile Dudevant (1804–1876), a celebrated French author of rustic novels.

CHAPTER TEN

1. Gilman here pokes fun at Karl Marx's base-to-superstructure framework wherein *all* cultural and social phenomena are said to arise necessarily from the underlying economic system.

2. Flora McFlimsy appears in William Allen Butler's *Nothing to Wear: An Episode of City Life* (New York: Rudd and Carleton, 1857). The opening stanza begins:

> Miss Flora M'Flimsey, of Madison Square,
> Has made three separate journeys to Paris,
> And her father assures me, each time she was there,
> That she and her friend Mrs. Harris
> (Not the lady whose name is so famous in history,
> But plain Mrs. H., without romance or mystery)

> Spent six consecutive weeks without stopping,
> In one continuous round of shopping;

The poem continues at length in like manner. James Barrie's novel, *A Window in Thurms* (London: Hodder & Stoghton, 1889), describes an invalid who sees the world only through a window:

> This is Jess's window. For more than twenty years she has not been able to go so far as the door, and only once while I knew her was she ben [sic] in the room. With her husband, Hendry, or their only daughter, Leeby, to lean upon, and her hand clutching her staff, she took twice a day, when she was strong, the journey between her bed and the window where stood her chair. . . . At this window she sat for twenty years or more looking at the world as through a telescope. . . .

CHAPTER ELEVEN

1. From the biblical parable of the talents, "His lord said unto him, well done thou good and faithful servant; thou hast been faithful over a few things, I will make thee ruler over many things; enter thou into the joy of the lord" (Gospel according to Matthew, chapter 25, verse 21, *The Interpreter's Bible*, Vol. 7 [New York: Abingdon Press, 1951: 560]).

CHAPTER TWELVE

1. Gilman's figures are precisely those reported also in *The World Almanac and Encyclopedia, 1913* (New York: Press Publishing Co., 1912: 244 and 260).

Index

About the Author and Editors

CHARLOTTE PERKINS GILMAN (1860–1935) was an eminent feminist sociologist and novelist, perhaps best known professionally for *Women and Economics* (1898) and, as a fiction writer, for her semiautobiographical story, *The Yellow Wallpaper* (1892). Recently issued editions of Gilman's *Herland* (1915) and *With Her in Ourland: Sequel to Herland* (1916) have attracted wide attention.

MICHAEL R. HILL is an interdisciplinary social scientist from the University of Nebraska-Lincoln who holds earned doctorates in both sociology and geography. He is the author of *Walking, Crossing Streets and Choosing Pedestrian Routes* (1984); *Archival Strategies and Techniques* (1993); editor of Harriet Martineau's *How to Observe Morals and Manners* (1989); and co-editor, with Mary Jo Deegan, of *Women and Symbolic Interaction* (1987) and Charlotte Perkins Gilman's *With Her in Ourland: Sequel to Herland* (Greenwood, 1997). He edits the journal, *Sociological Origins*. In 2000, Hill became Chair-elect of the History of Sociology section of the American Sociological Association.

MARY JO DEEGAN is Professor of Sociology at the University of Nebraska-Lincoln. Among her earlier publications are *Women and Disability* (1985); *Jane Addams and the Men of the Chicago School, 1892–1918* (1988); *American Ritual Dramas* (Greenwood, 1989); and *Women in Sociology: A Bio-*

Bibliographic Sourcebook (Greenwood, 1991). She is editor of *American Ritual Tapestry* (Greenwood, 1998); George Herbert Mead's *Play, School, and Society* (1999); *Essays in Social Psychology* (2001), *The Collected Works of Fannie Barrier Williams* (forthcoming); and co-editor, with Michael R. Hill, of *Women and Symbolic Interaction* (1987); and Charlotte Perkins Gilman's *With Her in Ourland: Sequel to Herland* (Greenwood, 1997).